"A deeply moving, genre-disrupting, passionate work, studded with gem-like lines, from the pioneering and always surprising Suniti Namjoshi."

—Ruth Vanita, author of *Love's Rite, Memory of Light*, and *A Slight Angle*

"It's full of wisdom and love, and sorrow, and loss. And yes, humour."

— Urvashi Butalia, author of *The Other Side of Silence*

"Suniti Namjoshi in this deeply soul-searching elegy for her beloved sister Bharati has gifted the world with a testimonial to what is the pure essence of truth and love."

—Revd Julie Lipp-Nathaniel

"Suniti Namjoshi will make you cry and smile, at times together. Like the swoop of a swallow, her prose glimmers and astounds. A luminous story of love, loss, and the fragility of relationships. And that fleeting thing, life."

—Bijal Vachharajani, children's author and editor

"A beautiful book about the vagaries and strengths of sisterly love. A many-faceted gem."

—Susan Varga, novelist, poet, biographer, author of *Rupture*

I0893620

Photo credit: Sharron Wallace Photography

Internationally acclaimed author Suniti Namjoshi is an important figure in contemporary literature in English. A writer of fables, poetry, satirical fiction and children's fiction, she has published over 30 titles in India, Australia, Canada and Britain. Born in Mumbai in 1941, she first wrote and published in India, then moved to Canada, and then to a small seaside village in the south-west of England with writer, Gillian Hanscombe. In 2023, she was elected a Fellow of the Royal Society of Literature. Her books include *Feminist Fables*, *Goja*, *Suki*, *Aesop the Fox* and *Blue and Other Stories* from Spinifex.

Other books by Suniti Namjoshi

Feminist Fables (1993)
St Suniti and the Dragon (1993)
Building Babel (1996)
Goja (2000)
The Fabulous Feminist (2012)
Blue and Other Stories (2012)
Suki (2014)
Aesop the Fox (2018)
The Good-Hearted Gardeners (2023)

O SISTER SWALLOW

An Elegy for Bharati Namjoshi

Suniti Namjoshi

SPINIFEX

We respectfully acknowledge the wisdom of Aboriginal and Torres Strait Islander peoples and their custodianship of the lands and waterways. The Countries on which Spinifex offices are situated are Djiru, Bunurong and Wurundjeri, Wadawurrung, Gundungarra and Noongar.

First published by Spinifex Press, 2024

Spinifex Press Pty Ltd
PO Box 200, Little River, VIC 3211, Australia
PO Box 105, Mission Beach, QLD 4852, Australia

women@spinifexpress.com.au
www.spinifexpress.com.au

Edited by Pauline Hopkins and Susan Hawthorne
Cover design by Deb Snibson
Typesetting by Helen Christie, Blue Wren Books
Typeset in Carrig
Printed and bound in Australia by Pegasus Media & Logistics

MIX
Paper from responsible sources
FSC® C008194
www.fsc.org

The paper in this book is FSC® certified. FSC® promotes environmentally responsible, socially beneficial and economically viable management of the world's forests.

A catalogue record for this book is available from the National Library of Australia

ISBN: 9781922964083 (paperback)
ISBN: 9781922964090 (ebook)

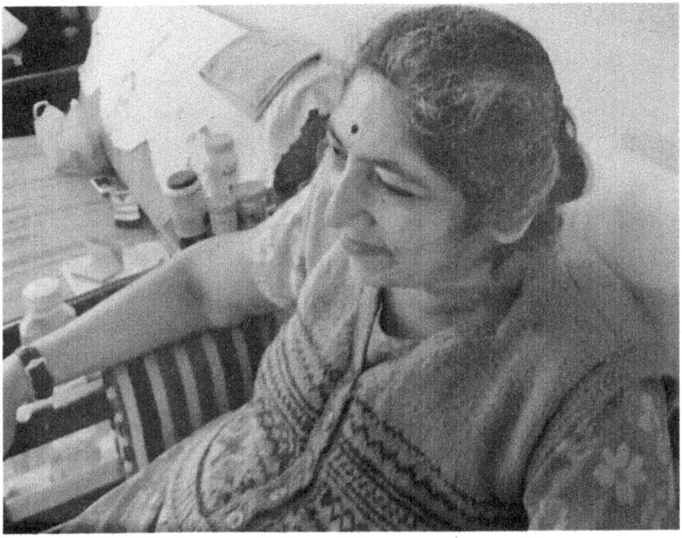

Bharati Namjoshi

(19 January 1945 – 2 November 2021)

Acknowledgements

'In the Garden Elsewhere' first appeared in *Converse: Contemporary English Poetry by Indians* edited by Sudeep Sen (Sutton, UK: Pippa Rann Books & Media, 2022). 'Snow White and Rose Green' first appeared in *From the Bedside Book of Nightmares* (Fredericton, Canada: Fiddlehead, 1984). 'The Mouse and the Lion' is from *Feminist Fables* (London: Sheba Feminist Publishers, 1981, rpt. 1884, with five new fables, 1990; Melbourne: Spinifex, 1993). 'The Dwarfs' is from *Sycorax: New Fables and Poems* (Penguin, India, 2006). 'Glass Coffins' is from *The Authentic Lie* (Frederiction, Canada: Fiddlehead, 1982).

I want to express my heartfelt gratitude to Sandra Lello, Ruth Vanita, Moya Wolfe, Farah Mendlesohn and Julie Lipp-Nathaniel, the five women who read through the initial manuscript and answered the question, "What did you wonder about or want to know after reading it?" I am also grateful to Urvashi Butalia, Renate Klein, Susan Hawthorne, and Pauline Hopkins for their careful reading of the text and their feedback. And as always, I have to thank my partner, Gill Hanscombe, for her encouragement and her infallible ear.

Contents

Swift Sparrows

... like the swift flight of a sparrow through the mead-hall ...

—The Venerable Bede

The sparrows have nested
in the hedgerow.
I do not disturb them.
It's not that I like
sparrows especially.
Their eggs are neither
black nor white,
just liberally speckled;
and when their scrawny fledglings
hatch
they won't know
life is fleeting.

1

Swallow, My Sister, O Sister Swallow!

Come away, my darling.

Suppose the family detached you and we sailed away in a pea-green boat. Suppose you shared with me all my experience of foreign parts and we shared with each other the known past and two different languages, both remembered. We would be unlikely companions, but friends, sisters. Suppose we allowed ourselves various suppositions. No hole in your heart. You would be whole and able. No hole in mine either, no remembered battering, long healed anyway. I too would be strong and capable. We would be the Two Sisters, Constellations in the Sky, wholly invincible. Why not allow ourselves a little glorification. It's not glory, I want – just understanding, and love. We had that, we loved one another, but the understanding was opaque. Shall we try again, Little One, Sister?

Let's start early. Why do little sisters want to copy their big sisters? I said I wanted to marry a millionaire. I was joking. Why would anyone want to do that? If they wanted millions, they could turn into millionaires themselves. You thought I was serious and said it was your ambition too. Were we very ragged?

Naked in our stupidities. Does love clothe us? I was amazed – not by your greed – you were never greedy. I was amazed by your heterosexuality. And you? I suppose you had to forgive my being a lesbian though I never felt you were forgiving me. I don't think it bothered you. What mattered was whatever kept me abroad, away from you. In your universe, the people you loved could do no wrong. Is that real forgiveness – when you feel there is nothing to forgive?

You were so very conventional – in some ways. Was that because you believed what people told you? Surely we all do that when we think what we're being told comes from an authoritative source. I firmly believe that the earth is round and goes around the sun though my eyes deny it.

At times what you said sounded like an almost exact repetition of something someone else had said. Perhaps being conventional is a way to be 'sane' or seem sane by fitting in with corroborative reality, agreeing with what people say is true. Like everyone else you picked and chose what to believe. I think you sometimes just said what you wished was true. Was that so wrong when allied to hope, to faith? You said that X didn't cheat you; he did what he did by accident, almost absentmindedly. Of course he cheated us. And you said that Y was quite fond of you. Really? He was an unrepentant bully – no question. Did you see something your elder sister didn't – their humanity? Did you fail to judge or refuse to judge? And was that kindness or was it a strategy? When one is weak, strategies are needed. Forgive me that I did not protect you better. I went off to the Wild West in order to protect myself. Let's share our lives and say what was left so explicitly unsaid; try to understand what we did not understand. How could we have loved each other so much and understood so little?

When you were quite small, say eight or nine, they took you to a psychiatrist in Bombay. I went along too. Perhaps they were taking me to the psychiatrist as well without telling me they were doing so. The psychiatrist asked, "Why do you speet?" You started giggling because he couldn't say 'spit' properly. I saw him write down: "Laughs for no reason."

Why did you spit? Was spitting a weapon – like biting? Doyou remember you bit me once when they were giving us a bath together? I don't know what came over you. You took out a tiny piece from my stomach. I was so surprised I forgot to howl.

You quite liked this 'Do you remember?' game, once you realised how it could be used. I'm sure you made up things. How could I deny what I could not remember? Hope you had fun. Were you telling me things that you wished had happened or that pointed to something else? Or just having fun? Are we doing that now in this remembrance of things past and things possible?

There are things I would like to apologise for, though for most of my stupidities – mostly impatience – you never reproached me. You laughed them away when I said, "Sorry." You said it didn't matter. But you did reproach me for going away, for doing it repeatedly, for visiting and then going away. First I'll apologise for the small things, for example, for giving you a haircut. I was eight, you were four. You were trusting. And I meant no harm. I had seen the barber put a sheet around someone sitting in a chair and snip away with a pair of scissors. I can still remember the green grass, the white sheet. I think our parents were horrified. We were not. But then why do I remember it?

I'm not sure you were a nice child. You threw things at people. You smiled at them sweetly and then threw things, like tins of talcum powder. But is this true or is it anecdotal? The way they tried to bind us with anecdotes and definitions, with lies and labels!

It's not true, is it, that you were conventional. Forgiving people is hardly commonplace. But some of your views were surely conventional – for example the literal belief in the Hindu pantheon. When I watched programmes with you about the gods on television, it seemed to me I was watching science fiction. Don't tell anyone. And why did you give credence to the claim that the Taj Mahal was really an ancient Hindu monument? I was scandalised. How right wing could you be in identifying with a nation, a religion and a class? How radical could I get? And do these divisions make sense? We all rely on a casual, consensual, makeshift reality and pick bits and pieces to shore up who we are or think we are or want to be.

You were unquestionably Indian – even your name made that clear. I was more of a one-world person before I left India, then more fiercely Indian in reaction to the West, and still later I acquired a couple of other nationalities and was more laid back about it all. You were definitely Hindu: did puja more or less every day, lit incense for the household gods. But then here, across the ocean, I have household gods too and light incense for them, though not as often as you did. The small Ganesh and Annapoorna were given to me by Ai. How could I not honour them? She was Grandma, she was the Matriarch, a roaring force like Niagara Falls. As for caste and class, I don't know whether you believed in the caste system. I think you had some idea that you weren't supposed to. The family was liberal, though perhaps not really. You were known as your grandparents' granddaughter and your father's daughter. So was I. It was helpful, it had some cachet. When I went to the West, I was suddenly nobody from nowhere. It was disconcerting, at times frightening, but also exciting. I felt so free. And I could always return to you at least once a year.

You stayed where you were, in one particular habitat. I took you for granted. When I came, I borrowed what I needed from you – needle and thread, your car – as though it was my god-given right as your elder sister – without so much as a word of thanks. Not that Marathi lends itself to thanks. And yet I was grateful with all my heart that you existed and were my sister and there for me.

Note that I refer to myself as your 'elder' sister, not 'older'. I was the eldest of the seventeen grandchildren; you the second eldest. But that gave us less status than it might have done. Probably because we were merely daughters of a daughter. Or because you had a hole in your heart and weren't as clever as the others, and I was just an unabashed lesbian, who didn't have the good sense or the good manners to lie. On the other hand, I was Ai's favourite, not because I was especially meritorious. I was her first grandchild and had spent a lot of time with her when I was little. You were not especially close to her, but I sometimes think that if she had not loved me, I would not have known how to love. You were treated with special consideration and well liked, even loved, by almost everyone. Perhaps we did matter. To each other, we did.

We started out together. You were only five – I was nine – when we were sent away to boarding school to be with a load of foreigners in the Himalayan foothills for nine months of the year. You came back with an American accent. It even affected the way you spoke Marathi and Hindi. Were we 'privileged'? It was a top school run by American missionaries for their own children, for children from the embassies and for a few Indians. They didn't convert the Indians in the school – that would have caused a scandal – but to be of any consequence one had to be Christian and American. Did any of it make sense to you – the Bible stories, the pink faces, the hair like metal? It didn't to me at first. And I don't think either of us 'appreciated' the splendour of our surroundings; the snow-clad Himalayan peaks in the distance, the oaks and the pines, the deodars and the rhododendrons, ferns and moss, cosmos growing wild on the hillside, which we uprooted like barbarians and flung into the valleys, yelling loudly that they were "parachute" plants. It was all very well – even the food was all right, though we complained because we thought we were supposed to – but neither of us wanted to be there.

You were not sent back again. They discovered – up there seven thousand feet above sea level – that you had a hole in your heart. No operation for that then. You had to wait until you were eighteen. Poor little mite. We were in the same dormitory, but I don't think our beds were next to each other. And we didn't eat at the same table. I understand now how miserable you must have been. I should have been a better elder sister, older sister, to you then, to you always. Being your elder gives me a certain status – and responsibility. At some point you started adding the appellation 'Tai' to my name. I've always suspected that it was to remind me of my duty to you. And the other grandchildren called you 'Tai' too. You liked that.

You never forgot your English. Many years later you could still speak it quite easily. But you stayed at home and did what studying you did in Marathi. Was that the main difference between us – that you learnt to do your thinking in Marathi, I learnt to do mine in English and that altered our perception of the world? After all, nothing colonises the brain more thoroughly than language.

They talk about sibling rivalry. I never felt it, and never sensed it in you. Was it because we were so different that we could not compete? I loved what was different about you and what was the same. We shared lots of genes. You once told a family friend that your sister had so many degrees that you didn't need any, you could always borrow one or two. And yet you worked valiantly to do your matriculation after The Operation. No easy feat. I admired you for that.

I was told that the hole in your heart had deprived you of oxygen while you were being born, and that therefore you were simple. When my partner first met you, I asked her to tell me how she saw you. I said I was too close to you to see you clearly, and tended to think of you as Miranda saying, "How beauteous mankind is!" She agreed you were simple and sheltered. Were you? You were never guilty of the crasser stupidities that are so plentiful in the wide world. I wrote a poem about us once that I never showed you. My writing was one of the things we did not share. I dedicated one of my books solely to you; you were unimpressed. That was salutary.

Sisters often borrow each other's clothes. You liked the pastel colours of the Chanderi saris. I didn't like those. They were hard to wear and puffed out. I liked the gorgeous colours of the heavy Kanjivarams. You said that we looked alike, but that you were fairer. You pinched my saris on the grounds that the colours suited you better. I was indulgent and said everything suited you better, but then I didn't care about saris. We could borrow each other's talents. You could teach me to be kind and forgiving, and content with my lot. What could I teach you, my darling? How to be ferocious? Fight battles? And quaver in the dark? You were braver than me. To live so close to death always, to hear your heart thudding away inside you, that would take courage. At the last, when we were both pretending that you would get better, I saw the shadow of death cross your face, and you saw that I saw, even though we talked of your birthday and whether I would return for it.

So then it's hardly surprising if you often talked of The Operation when you were taken to Copenhagen and had the hole stitched up, and if you counted that as the great event in your life. Permission to live is a great event. It meant you could have a long life, and you did have a long life as these things go – seventy-six years – but not long enough. After the operation your handwriting changed, it stopped being shaky. I remember waiting for the plane that was bringing you back. It seemed to me that it was flying through the skies for that sole purpose – to bear you home. India was still home to me then. I had chocolate mints ready for you. I didn't stop to think whether you would want chocolate mints after a heart operation.

There were things that you wanted me to tell you, things you thought I knew or remembered because I was older than you, and I wouldn't and didn't because I thought such truths were too harsh, for example, that before Dad was killed our parents hadn't been getting along. You thought our parents were above reproach. I thought they were human beings, not the god-like creatures we wanted them to be. Perhaps both ways of thinking are, in their way, respectful.

There's a letter from Dad to our mother dated the 21st of September, 1938. He's twenty-one, she's eighteen. He's impatient, impetuous and very much in love.

Impatient: – *"Those damned mails are late by 72 hours. It means that I won't have any news from you till tomorrow evening."*

Wondering: – *"What do you think of the central European situation? I am certain there is going to be* <u>*no*</u> *war. How would you like my joining the Reserve of Indian Air Force officers? I am not anxious to spill my blood for the Britishers but I would like to do it for the defence of India ...*

I have been here since the 17th: it is as well that you are not waiting for me at the other end, otherwise I do not know how very restless I would be. But it is only a few days & then there need be no waiting. Of course, I'll do my best to come over, but that was not what I was thinking of; I was picturing myself as an instructor and you my beloved, my companion for life."

Ardent, demanding, teasing: *"What are you doing now? Are you writing to me? How is your little finger? Have you started to play tennis? Do you go riding? I mean to take it up seriously for otherwise I will feel stupid or look stupid before you ... The only thing you may beat me badly with would be with your brains – but you so often forget them at home!"*

And filled with the dream of a life together: *"How long does it take you to write a three page letter? This one took over three hours – for I was half dreaming & half awake."*

They are so young, almost children. And it breaks my heart as I, an old woman in her eighties, read and transcribe his letter. She outlived him by sixty-five years. He was thirty-six when his plane crashed, less than half your age or mine.

What can I tell you about him that I remember as a child? That he was kind. Admired by people for winning all the air races and doing big game hunting and being good at tennis. That he told good stories even though they were repetitive. That his plane crash doing aerobatics in a tiny trainer aircraft, which got caught in someone else's jet stream, made sensational headlines. That I grieved and grieved and had a recurrent dream in which he came back and then I woke up. I remember what he was like in relation to me. I cannot remember what he was like in relation to you, though I try. For that forgive me. Were you more orphaned than me because I remember more? Four years isn't much of a head start. Then one day you told me that you knew quite a lot already.

You always assumed that my friends were your friends and this included partners. And those closest to me were. They sent you bird calendars and postcards knowing how much you mattered to me. You realised gradually that I had a life here which might militate against my having a life there. Initially my being away didn't matter so much because you were in better health and could do more things; and anyway, I came back once a year. It was when your health got worse and worse that the crucial question arose: "How will you survive?"

I usually knew less than I thought I did – the disadvantage of considering myself quite perspicacious. I should have seen more clearly what was happening to you while I wasn't there. I didn't. It was so gradual and perhaps I didn't want to.

You always knew more than people thought you did – the advantage of not being considered as clever as other people. For instance, you realized gradually that I had a partner, she had a son. When a granddaughter was born on whom I doted, I showed you her picture. You were polite, but not really interested. Because you felt that somehow my life here was not as valid as your life there? Or because all you wanted – and needed – was for me to be with you?

I don't think that you felt my life was less important and that as an unmarried woman it was my duty to return home to look after an ailing sister and mother. There was only your need. My saying to you, "My home is always open to you," must have sounded hollow in your ears. This was not an environment you could survive in. There's a crucial line in a sequence of poems my partner, Gill, and I wrote together:

"The family not for joining."

She had visited a couple of times, but it was made clearer and clearer that this was not a good idea. Your habitat was no good for me, and in mine you would not survive.

We should have talked more, but all we did was play cards. What could we have said? Was there censorship going on? Why couldn't we talk? Shall we make up for it now? What will you tell me? You will tell me about bird life. You sometimes did. You never visited me here. This land, this landscape is so unfamiliar to you. Shouldn't there be a bridge from the known to the unknown? I remember an aunt once opened the freezer compartment and told her little daughter that that was what it was like where I lived. She was joking. I lived in Canada then. England or Canada, it was all far away and equally exotic. I remember you told a doctor friend that I lived in London. My darling, there is a difference between London and England. If I had pointed that out, you would have smiled and nodded; after all, what difference did it make?

And yet, I remember you asked about my life here, just as I asked about yours when I wasn't there.

Suppose you had visited. I would have had to wait on you. You needed help, and you were used to servants. I would have got cross. Then I would have said, "Sorry," and you would have forgiven me whether I said sorry or not. I wanted to show you the birds in this garden, just ordinary birds – robins, blackbirds, blue tits, coal tits, magpies, wood pigeons – but unfamiliar to you. I'll show them to you now, just as you showed me the sunbirds, the bulbuls, the tailorbirds and the grey tits where you were. We'll do all the things we never did, and talk about some of the things we managed to do. Do you remember the flapping of wings as the storks took off over our heads? I'm glad we shared that, and going out to lunch, just the two of us, and eating tandoori pomfret? Walking about in the university gardens when you could still walk easily and listening to the seven sisters chattering in the trees? Do you remember the time we came across a tamarind tree that was so bountiful that it had thrown down scores of tamarinds, ripe ones, and left many more within easy reach. We gathered them up in handfuls and took them home.

About my going away – you never understood it. Many years later I gave you a film about migratory birds. There was no hidden message. I thought you'd like the film, but you looked at me mildly and said, "The birds come and the birds go, the birds come and the birds go. So what?" Was I equally inexplicable? Should I have stayed with you and helped to look after you for the rest of your life? If I had cried out, "What about my life?" you would have said, "What's that to me if I cannot share it!" Only you didn't say it. We were both silent.

The repeated abandonment – you forgave even that. But that tacit reproach, sometimes not so tacit, always hung in the air: *Don't go? Why must you go?*

I could ask you that now. I was older. I had precedence. Why did you go first? Of course I can follow, and will follow inevitably. Will you look back?

> *Swallow, my sister, O sister swallow ...*
> *What wilt thou do when the summer is shed?*
>
> —*Itylus*, Swinburne

2

The Stage Set

When you were very little I remember playing hide and seek with you. You closed your eyes and declared that if you couldn't see me, I couldn't see you. Now neither of us can see the other. Is that true? Should we start with the last days, both of us aware they were slipping by: you, unable to eat, uncomplaining, and the two of us talking about the birds we could see, the parrots, the kites, the pigeons? We could swim through the ocean of memory. We could be dolphins in an unpolluted ocean. Why not, even though the ocean is cluttered with the debris of half remembered things.

And there's another problem: how do we talk to each other without referring to, or sometimes even talking about, the figures in the background – the family, the friends, the connections? They wouldn't like it, might not like it, and I don't want to embarrass them. About some of them we might disagree radically. According to you everyone was wonderful. That's one way of looking at things. And it's true that you were much loved. You had this notion about yourself that you could walk unscathed through the world: no dog would ever attack you, no human being harm you. It's also true that even the most ferocious dogs became docile when you approached; but, my darling it's not sensible to be so trusting of everyone.

I'll turn the family into Cloudy Figures, all except those about whom there is no ambivalence. But there is always ambivalence. People are never fixed, never consistent. It's only convenience and our use of nouns that makes them seem so. The cloudiness will work. We need not disagree. And what we say to each other need not trouble anyone. That was part of the censorship when we talked. There were things we did not want to say to each other, people we did not want to talk about. For my part, I did not want to implicate you in anything. You lived among them – the Cloudy Figures. I suspect your reasons were similar.

The Cloudy Figures impacted on us. How could they not – that extended family with houses next to each other and so clannish that friends were almost unnecessary, at least peripheral. At the head were Ai and Baba, our grandparents, gradually losing both wealth and power, though, after Independence, Baba joined the Congress Party and for a time had some power. By 1947 most of the princely states had already been merged. The privy purse they had been compensated with dwindled in a climate of roaring inflation, and in 1971 was abolished altogether. Giving land to the Bhoodan Movement and the land acts didn't help, but we never heard Ai or Baba complain. They remained who they were and embraced us all, though during their lifetimes the land did not turn into gold. Their children were the princelings, our mother and her four younger brothers. And then came our lot, seventeen grandchildren, all jumbled together, cousins and siblings, jostling and pushing, and eventually their children, the Cloudy Young Ones. Family politics was in the air we breathed, but as the seventeen of us grew older, most of us acknowledged kinship and tried to hurt each other as little as possible.

You were the most vulnerable of us all. Among the cousins there was one who visited you often. The two of you were the same age and called each other "January" and "February" because those were the months in which you were born. I was glad for your sake that you had each other. I would not have willingly offended her, and yet I did. It was stupid, not malicious, and one more thing for which I have to ask your forgiveness. You had just had your operation for breast cancer and were more fragile than ever. She came in her car to take you for a drive, but then she made you get out of the car saying she didn't have enough petrol and that the two of you should use your car and your driver. She had done this before. And I was angry, seeing you standing there trembling in the middle of the road. I asked if she would like some money for petrol. She said, "Yes," and I gave her some, which she later returned. But I think she felt insulted and probably she visited you less often. I would not have harmed you for the world, and yet I did you some harm.

Or on another occasion, you introduced me to someone you had met among the neighbours. She had just got into the Indian Administrative Service (from which I had resigned some years before). I did not congratulate her as profusely as she expected, and that was stupid. You could have done with a friend or an acquaintance. You had some friends from the World Wildlife Fund, but most of your social life was within the circle of the extended family, as it was for many of the others. Claustrophobic perhaps, but also supportive.

You and one of the Cloudy Young Ones used to enjoy going out to lunch together. You paid and why not, you were much older; but when that was commented on, the lunches stopped. There's a cliché: if America sneezes, the world catches a cold. Well, if anyone sneezed, you caught pneumonia. You were at the mercy of other people's actions. No wonder if for you survival was a primary concern. It happened sometimes that the Clan was careless, but it was also protective. I thought of you sometimes as a bird who could only live in one particular habitat.

That was the setting: the princely state and the apportioned farmlands a couple of hours away in a motor car and the houses in the city next to each other or nearby. And for the two of us the setting had a focus: the 'drawing room' in our mother's house. We will call her M, your mother and mine – it's easier that way. And we'll keep that name for the stage set. It was only later that I realised that in British English 'Drawing Room' was short for 'Withdrawing Room'. There was no withdrawing there, it was sometimes called the 'hall' – it was nothing so grand.

With the merger of the princely states the status of the nobles and notables diminished considerably; among themselves, though, many observed the niceties of rank. The kind of namaskar each was entitled to and from whom was calculated to the last millimetre. I suppose people felt that they could only preserve their own position if they scrupulously observed everyone else's. "For how art thou a king / But by fair sequence and succession?" (*Richard II*, 2, i).

Rank was dependent on a number of things, and even children were instructed in advance. I wondered if doing an overly respectful namaskar to someone who wasn't entitled to it was worse than not bowing down (to the right degree) to someone who was entitled to it? We sometimes got it wrong, especially after Independence when many of the men wore Nehru caps and the same sort of khadi clothes. We were corrected, but not scolded.

I worked out some of the factors that mattered. Kinship to Shivaji Maharaj was important, no matter how long ago. Then the number of gun salutes a state was entitled to also counted. Twenty one was terrific. None at all – Ai and Baba had none at all – was much less good. After all, there were five hundred and sixty-five or so princely states. Some were enormous like Kashmir and Hyderabad and others were tiny. I don't think the prestige of having guns fired conferred anything other than itself.

'Toys for the boys,' I thought, but I didn't say anything. Caste and sub-caste also mattered and ancestry. The further back you could go the better. I remembered the third book of *Gulliver's Travels*, but kept that to myself.

I don't think you questioned any of this as much. You were clear that privilege implied obligations. Elder sisters, for example, were supposed to look after younger ones. And you quite liked it when the Cloudy Cousins acknowledged your place as the second oldest in our generation. Well, I won't tease. It's hard to refuse privilege when it is being offered. And, of course, we were often unaware of it. When people were nice to us, we assumed it was because they were nice. Or we were nice? Or only well connected?

Once when we were shopping on Main Street, you stumbled and fell. I wasn't strong enough to hold you up, and the driver had gone away to park somewhere. People rushed to help. They were kind. Would they have been kind if you had looked poor? That was another factor that conferred rank – if you came from a rich state, that counted for quite a lot; and also who was married to whom, and who your cousins were and your uncles and aunts and the exact nature of the relationship, and, of course, beyond that, who their cousins were. It was confusing, but people kept track.

A degree of humility was definitely in order. And there was humility. I saw it most clearly in Ai and Baba, in the way they greeted people. It was there particularly in Baba. I never saw him angry, never heard him being rude to anybody. It was his most shining virtue. And it was odd that, because he was the source of the wisps of royalty with which the rest of us covered ourselves. To be fair, all of us were haunted by a faded grandeur in varying degrees – even me, even you. If asked where you were from, you always said you came from that state. And I confess that I was angry (kept that to myself too) when people were less respectful than they used to be to Ai and Baba.

Nevertheless, the stage set we occupied was only a middle class living room with a couple of sofas, bits of furniture and a television set. A couple of paintings hung on the wall and inevitably a portrait of Shivaji Maharaj, not looking at us so much, as out at the world, or more probably thinking his own unknowable thoughts.

M controlled the action from a particular corner. You were a character that was always there, not necessarily important – more like furniture; and I was a character that was always exiting – like a footman or a messenger. We sat on an ottoman playing simplified bridge and being distracted by the wildlife pictures on the playing cards. You liked the birds best. I liked them too, but I liked the butterflies as well. We didn't say much and we knew that we weren't of much consequence as we did not contribute to the glory of the family. People came and went, Cloudy Figures: reminiscing princesses, old friends of M's, some kind, some not so kind, friends of friends, and relatives, and relatives of relatives. Our income had made us middle class people, but sometimes we found it difficult to remember that.

People walked about the stage, drank tea, gossiped, sat around and were conscious of who they were and who everyone else was in relation to them. Once I heard a distantly related Cloudy Figure claim that his rank and status (and wealth) were earned. They were the result of the merit points accumulated in a past life. How deal with such inculcated smugness? Did you question the arbitrary order? Or did you just see them as the nobility practising *noblesse oblige* – sometimes? Surely, we were both complicit, even when we were kind, no, especially perhaps when we were kind. Being gracious was a part of good manners.

Gossip went on too. We were told that a spiteful figure had called you a moron and me a lesbian. I hope it didn't bother you. It seemed to me that if that was the worst that could be said about us, we were doing pretty well. We were not the villains or the heroes of this Drawing Room Drama. We were the extras or the groundlings. And we were innocuous. You couldn't fight and I was a non-entity because of my absence. Somewhere in all the scrabbling for position, for power, sometimes even for sheer survival, somewhere in this jungle, there must have been room for sanctuary, even grace. Did we find it in a deck of playing cards?

We were often seen as a pair. Our first names half-rhymed, and our pet names rhymed perfectly. The two sisters would do this or do that – especially at festivals when we would have to follow the rites, do puja, bless whoever had to be blessed or in turn get blessed.

M was an agnostic or an atheist, and didn't celebrate the festivals much, but the culture penetrated anyway. Ai celebrated nearly all the festivals and because of her I quite liked them, but I had my reservations. When we had to do the rite for blessing the appropriate Cloudy Figures for Bhau Beej at Diwali, I was amazed by how coolly some of them could sit there and get blessed after having just done a tricky bit of legerdemain to do with money and land dealings. You didn't mind. I did, but I fitted in. I had similar reservations about tying a rakhi around a male wrist and therefore presumably asking for protection. Was I too bloody minded to think I needed protection? Like you, though not as much, I needed it all right, but I was wary.

I checked the internet to see if there was a festival that celebrated the bond between sisters. They just went on about Raksha Bandhan and the tie between a brother and a sister; there was only one entry asking that it be extended to include the bond between sisters. Who cares? I care. We didn't live inside a vacuum, or inside a fridge. Where did we live in relation to each other? There, in that relationship, that connection between us, and that also matters.

Do you remember the time I borrowed a set of gold bangles from you for some occasion or another? These were proper bangles, not just an ornate piece of glitter like a rakhi. I happened to say I quite liked them. You wanted to give them to me at once. I touched your cheek and said, "My darling, it's for an elder sister to give her younger sister jewellery, not the other way round." M saw to it that all your jewellery went to someone else including trinkets I had given you. Perhaps just as well. I would not have been able to wear your jewellery once you were gone. I had my own jewellery, which Ai had given me. Some of which had belonged to M; she had left it behind when she married Dad. That some of that jewellery came to me and skipped M must have been difficult. There's a different narrative when women and their relationships to each other are foregrounded. Different, yes, but not less painful.

Of the festivals, you liked Ganesh Chaturthi best. You and the driver set up a Ganapati, not quite on the stage set, but on the veranda outside. I loved your pleasure in decorating a place fit for the god. Of the festivals I liked Sankranti best. It almost always fell on the fourteenth of January because it was a solar festival and only four days away from your birthday. I was almost always there for it. Ai used to have special til-gul made with pieces of pistachio and cashew embedded in the spiky white sugar. There would be a bowl of the ordinary til-gul containing sesame seeds on the Stage Set. When people gave some to each other – usually seniors to juniors – they would say: "तीळगुळ घ्या आणि गोड गोड बोला! – Take the til-gul and speak sweetly." I thought privately that they said this because more often than not they didn't speak sweetly. Marathi isn't a sweet language. It lends itself more to sarcasm and irony. And yet, you were never sarcastic or ironic.

Time rushed through the stage set like a steady wind. The cast was diminished, new figures appeared; but the change was slow, almost imperceptible. Sometimes when I came after a year, I noticed that people had become more like themselves, had turned into caricatures. On this stage set, the characters were their own audience, and the performers were the characters. Did you wonder what sort of a play we were in? A domestic drama? A sitcom? A melodrama? Perhaps it wasn't a play at all, but an MGM film with a cast of thousands, or a soap opera, or a chess board. Who moved the pieces? Perhaps we were all in a different play. But on that particular stage set, surely M's version prevailed – just as Prospero's does in *The Tempest*. She must have had her own set of memes – bits of imagery – with which to create her own play in what was, after all, her own living room.

Towards the end you said to me, "What should I do when M is no longer there to look after me? Should I die?" For you to feel that you would cease to exist should she vanish ... that, indeed, is a sign of power – at least over you. When she died, she gave away the house. No more stage set. Like Prospero she could say:

> *Our revels now are ended. These our actors,*
> *As I foretold you, were all spirits and*
> *Are melted into air, into thin air ...*
>
> —*The Tempest IV, i*

Nevertheless, the stage set was not the universe. It had wings: the houses of the Cloudy Uncles, on the roadside the frangipani trees M had planted and which the bulbuls and the grey tits liked, and further afield – the university gardens, the city, the state, the world. Your mobility was limited, but there were other settings, and going for drives was one of your favourite pastimes.

On that particular stage our lines were limited, but what we say to each other now can be seen as an extended aside while the drama plays on. An aside – out of the margins – gives voice to the marginalised. It comments on the action, and at least suggests an alternative plot. Away with the sitcom or the drawing room drama or the soap opera. This is between the two of us. We are offstage in a space of our own, though it's hard to reach you. I am shouting now as loudly as I can. I am trying to tell you how much you mattered.

3

Rose Green

Sailing away in a pea-green boat was never an option. Life is lived in a certain locale, a milieu, among other people. Besides, owls are the one species of bird you don't like. Why? Too sinister for you? I woke up once with a small owl sitting on my pillow. We frightened each other equally. When I had put on my glasses and pulled myself together, I picked it up and set it down in the fork of a tree where it would be safe till it was dark again. I decided it was Athene's messenger and that my work would go well. You told me that you had seen green owls. Green owls? I looked them up in bird books. I even searched the internet. Not to be found. Is this talk about owls irrelevant, to be excluded from a book that seeks to – that seeks to – find you. It's hard to know what matters and what does not. You were not just to be found among the Cloudy Figures. We found each other in bird talk as well.

Someone once told me that violins are made by carving the wood and then throwing away the carved portions. These details then are shavings that are somehow an essential part of the process. Or perhaps what I'm trying to explore is my relationship to you, what it means to be sisters, what we were to each other as sisters. I almost wish that Swinburne's lines about the swallow had not come into my head. It's not a happy story. There are different versions, and so you could be the nightingale and I could be the swallow or the other way about. Or we could just be a pair of swallows and forget about the myth or about being people. Some say it was Philomel who had her tongue cut out. Others say it was Procne. Well, we're talking now.

I'll tell you something I never told you. (There must be zillions of things I never told you, and zillions of things you never told me.) When I was teaching English Literature to undergraduate students I'd sometimes set them a question asking them to describe the parallels and contrasts between two characters. After a while I stopped doing it, because I realised that you couldn't have contrasts unless there were parallels. What is the point in comparing and contrasting two completely unlike things, for example a tea cake and a telephone? What about us?

Here's the story I never showed you.

SNOW WHITE AND ROSE GREEN

Once upon a time there were two sisters and one got married and one didn't. Or, once upon a time there were two piglets and one went to market and one didn't, or, one was straight and one wasn't. The point is whatever they did or failed to do, they were a great disappointment to their poor mother. Luckily for them, the two sisters loved one another. When they saw that their mother was growing more and more unhappy, they proposed to her that she cut them in half and out of the two good halves make one splendid one. Their mother refused in high indignation, but she was so wretched that the dutiful daughters went to a surgeon. The surgeon obligingly sawed them in half, then interchanged halves and stuck them together. But there were still two of them. This was a problem. So they went back home and said to their mother, "Now choose the good one." But their mother was furious that they had even thought of such a scheme. "You did it to mock me," she told them angrily. "You are both bad children." When the two sisters heard her say this, the Good One wept, but the Bad One smirked.

When I wrote this I thought of myself as Rose Green, but you can be Rose Green if you like, we can take turns. Or you can be Snow White, with me being Rose Red, and only a little less sweet. It says in that story that no harm ever came to them, and a guardian angel, who looks after good children, watched after them. One married a bear and the other the bear's brother. Seriously? Oh all right, princes in disguise. And they lived with their mother who took care of them and of everything else. You can be Snow White if you like, but I am Rose Green and I'm running away in a pea-green boat, with a five pound note, to sink or swim or stay afloat – just as I like! Stop laughing. Oh well, I did that to make you laugh.

Suppose the difference between us is that you wanted to be normal, to conform; I didn't, couldn't. You got married. It didn't work out. I've lived with my partner for over thirty-five years and my life isn't all that different from anyone else's. It could be in a soap opera. I suspect no one can conform. As for your wanting to conform and my not wanting to, that's all rubbish. We wanted what we wanted and sometimes we got it wrong. We never spoke of it much.

You always liked sour things, also sweet things, but sour things better. I was the reverse. Did that make us different? Is it a difference worth talking about?

And how did we both end up being partial to birds, delighting in their flight, their song, even though oceans separated us? You could recognize some birds by the sounds they made even though they were hidden high in the trees. We were lucky we shared that just by chance. I don't think there's a gene for liking birds.

We were the same and different. Agreed.

One difference did matter: I was healthy and you often weren't. It was hard for me to understand what being in pain was like, how being helpless felt. It made me care less, that is, both negligent and uncaring. For that forgive me. There was so much more that I only guessed at, but couldn't wholly understand – the discipline required to be a good invalid, a forbearing patient. You were supremely good at that – to a fault. Once you fell and broke your collarbone. The servants called me. I said it was nothing, no harm had been done, because that was what I wanted to believe. You must have suffered through the night. The next day the X-ray revealed the damage done. Or sometimes you would tell me that your back ached. I would just look at you foolishly, not knowing what to do.

You went through a phase of trying magnet therapy. I didn't know whether it was useful or not. I didn't seem to know anything much. When your feet began to swell, I begged you to use bandages or stockings because that's what the doctors said you were to do. And when you had cancer and they did a mastectomy, I tried not to tell you that it had been cancer, but you knew. You always knew and you endured it all. You had more than thirty medicines you had to take every day. One day when the nurse couldn't do it, I had to try to sort them into their proper boxes for morning, noon and night. I was terrified that I would get it wrong. Despite my ignorance, I should have tried harder to understand your medical problems. On my report card the teacher would have written: "Could do better."

Another difference between us: one little piggy went abroad, and one little piggy stayed at home. That made it more and more difficult to find a language in which we could speak to each other.

If our views of the universe we inhabited differ so radically and of the people therein, should I try to convince you that I am right? Should you try to convince me that I am mistaken?

If I can't know who you really were, why don't we make up straightforward lies, or straightforward truths, whatever – as the young people say. I'll make them up, you can correct me as I go along. For example:

I had a sister once. She was beautiful.

Yes, but my teeth stuck out. I had to have braces when I was little.

She was fair.

Yes, I was, wasn't I? You were relatively dark.

Being unpleasant?

Just truthful.

Would you rather have had your multiverse sister – able, capable, a society hit, and glamorous? And not me, as I'm neither sociable, nor blindingly beautiful?

And now I hear you turning dangerous. What about you? Would you rather have had your twin? Difficult, unsociable, not especially beautiful, but clever like you?

We never said those things, thought those things. I did want a twin once, but it was only because of the age difference. And if you had wanted an elder sister who could have discussed saris more competently, I can understand that. All forgotten and forgiven. I forgive you. I mean the other way about. Oh this is silly.

I thought I was supposed to look after you, but I did notice sometimes that you looked after me. Somehow, the things I liked to eat were always on hand when I happened to visit. You used to like sitting in the sunlight, when it wasn't too hot, shelling peas, and even *harbara* in the winter. You liked eating the tender green peas and the *harbara* kernels, but there was always enough for me. And do you remember the time you carried a tacky plastic bottle under your finery to a posh wedding and I asked in my lofty elder sisterly way, "Why on earth are you carrying that around?" You replied meekly, "It's for you, in case you get thirsty." My darling, little sister, what was I to say to that? You were so dear – a sweetie, except, of course, when you were not – but that happened seldom. You shamed me with your simplicity.

After a few years, you were sent away with me again, this time to an experimental school in the deep south. This was also a good school, but very different. J. Krishnamurti used to come to the school for a couple of months every year. The landscape consisted of green paddy fields in a valley surrounded by a ring of small hills on which the boulders looked huge in comparison. Instead of piano lessons, there was south Indian classical music, and the food was south Indian vegetarian, not western. We could study as we wished and ask whatever questions we wanted to. At the time there were no regular classes or internal exams. Most of the teachers were Indian, as were the students. We were taught in English, both schools had excellent libraries and some of the teachers were kind. Those things were the same – and the fact that you were miserable. And once again I failed you. You left after one term, and I left as soon as I could after getting through a school leaving exam. I don't think anyone intended to be cruel. These were thought to be good schools. The first was American as opposed to one based on a British model, and supposedly 'freer', less rigid, less formal – no uniforms for example. And at the second school we were expected to think for ourselves, question our conditioning. I suspect that a little less freedom might have suited some of the students.

Years later, those of us from the second school who lived locally would meet sometimes. When I happened to be around, I would take you along to the school gatherings. Once I asked you how you'd got on. You said, "All of you talked so much and so loudly that I couldn't get a word in." True enough. We were all very full of ourselves. Excusable in the others perhaps, but not in me.

Do I always have to be the one to ask forgiveness? Didn't you ever do anything horrid to me? What about the time you ordered some fish and wouldn't give me any because I hadn't paid for it? I was very nice about it. You never did it again.

But always there remains your chief charge against me. I had told you once that the West was a terrible place for old people, and that in my old age I would return to spend my last days with you. One day, you asked me happily, "So, when are you coming back to settle down?" And I had to tell you that I had a life in the West and that probably I was never coming back. I remember I said it casually as though it was something obvious. I realised later how hard that must have hit you.

My darling, I have some understanding now of all the disappointment, the life-threatening disappointment, you suffered. That you did need looking after was clear. I had made a promise and it was a lie. There was a truth also that I never told you: the element you lived in was noxious to me. I could only live in it for brief periods of time. Were you a bird of the air then, and was I fish who had to live underwater? Were we so alien that we did not even belong to the same family, never mind species? Birds and fish do belong to the same class. Oh this is nonsense. I'm making a stupid joke because I looked up Animal Classification. And anyway, it was I who kept flying to and fro, to and fro, endlessly.

If two plants that are the same species grow in different climates, do they then grow differently? I got acclimatised to living in the West, you to living at home in a highly protected environment. I could not bear the heat very well, you didn't like air conditioning. We were lucky we did not lose our kinship. You never made any remarks about NRI's – effete non-resident Indians – it wouldn't have occurred to you. When germs I would formerly have thrown off without a thought now attacked me mercilessly if I wasn't careful, you merely made sure I had boiled drinking water.

4

Tinker, Tailor, Painter, Writer

We were the wrong class to be tinkers or tailors. And certainly daughters couldn't be any such thing. Even the boys had restrictions. They were not supposed to go 'into service'. What were they supposed to live on then when there were ceilings on how much land could be held, when the tenancies had vanished with the tenants demanding land for themselves and there were no revenues to speak of? True, our poor father, however glamorous and dashing a figure he cut as a test pilot, had been 'in service'. Mother had in some ways 'married beneath her', and then Dad's plane had crashed. We were not only aristocratic, or half-aristocratic, we were also relatively impoverished, rather like Mrs Bennett's daughters. I don't think you ever read Jane Austen, but you'd have understood the kind of life she describes.

Our mother's generation was too enmeshed in feudalism to understand what capitalism meant or to understand the implications of the Industrial Revolution. Perhaps to them it just meant electric lights and pretty motor cars. When the world changed they didn't know what they were supposed to do or who they were supposed to be. Farmers rather than landowners? But they didn't know how to farm. They hadn't been trained to do anything much – just to be princes, which under the British, given the resident in the palace, was more a matter of appearance than reality. And yet, there's the scrap of an undated letter from one of the Cloudy Uncles (as a boy) to Dad, which gives a sense of how carefree they were – at least at times. In it he wants to know from Dad how to train a kite as he has found a fledgling; and he's writing because when he had asked his sister to ask Dad, she had said she wouldn't because it would only give him (Dad) a swollen head. Silly perhaps, but innocent, at least harmless.

As for M, our mother the princess, she had given up all for love and turned herself into a figure so romantic that in her own eyes she transcended mere feudalism. Something like that. I don't know. In a way all this was play-acting, in 'real life' such roles often lacked relevance. It was hard for that generation. They saw themselves as kshatriyas, and as we were brought up in that milieu, we had a fair idea of what that meant – being brave, never crying or showing weakness, never putting up with an insult and always being up for a battle. I questioned some of this later; but we were conditioned by the set up. Technically we were brahmins. Dad's family was mostly gone and he hadn't known much about being a brahmin. Too westernized. He and his older brother had had an English governess. I don't think I ever heard you tell anyone you were a brahmin. I didn't either. But then, I suppose, in a caste-conscious society, nobody needed to say anything. Everyone kept tabs on everyone, knew their ancestry and how they were related to everyone else. A little forgetfulness might have been helpful.

Our lot, that is the Seventeen Grandchildren, the Cloudy Cousins, were willing to work. I remember when, for a brief time, M got you a job in a nursery, how proud you were, how filled with a sudden self-respect. I hadn't realised till then that accepting your limitations was hard for you – you did it so well.

What about Painter and Writer then – that is you and me? A little ladylike painting – dabbling – was permissible. As for writing, spending time on a musical instrument would have been preferable. The important thing was not to take it seriously. A serious writer was someone aristocrats patronised, also a serious painter; and in any case it was not something a woman – any woman – could do seriously. But we were serious. Both of us. And the Cloudy Figures? They forgave us or ignored us or smiled at how seriously we took ourselves. We were sometimes referred to as Painter and Writer with the 'would-be' left out with kindly forbearance. It angered me. I'm not quite sure how much. And you? You went on painting. Like you, I went on writing. In time, one of the Cloudy Cousins, the one who had an MA in literature, took to reading my work, demanded it hot off the computer. I don't think she realised how much that warmed my heart. Like you, she too is gone.

There's also this to be said. When Ai asked me what I wanted be – I had already thrown away one good job – I said I wanted to be a poet. To this she replied, "Ah, that requires a deep understanding of the human heart." That scared me. At the time I didn't want to venture in too deeply. I have tried since.

Don't forget that even Jane Austen had to cover up her writing and couldn't tell everyone to be quiet because she was concentrating. Let's look at our lives through a Jane Austen lens. It might be useful. Do you remember Elizabeth saying to Lady What-was-her-name, "I am a gentleman's daughter"? You don't, and it doesn't matter. The point is, did we bank on our status – what we had of it? I suppose we did, but not to the point of despising our own talents. "It is a truth universally acknowledged ..." – Jane Austen on the marriage market, being ironic, with the ironies doubled and tripled and multiplied. That was the acceptable option, though I expect we both knew we were not marketable. I smoked, went about in jeans and slacks, did what I liked and was altogether unsuitable. When it turned out that I was also clever and had got a most sought after job, the difficulties became insurmountable. What man wants to marry a clever woman, unless, of course, she's clever enough to convince him that she's isn't? For me it didn't matter, because I didn't want to marry a man, and at the time any other options were unthinkable. You did want to marry. And when it looked as though no one was doing anything about it, you ran away by bus to the small town where the farmlands were. That focused attention. Something was arranged. It didn't work out. I am so sorry. I should have warned you, I should have helped. But what could I have done? You weren't listening.

And to all this what would Jane Austen have said? I do not think she would have approved of me. And about wanting to be a writer and taking myself seriously? "Not seemly," she would have said. "Not in keeping with propriety." But that's what she did! More power to her arm and three cheers from a safe distance. We women should support one another. I'm not sure you and I supported each other, not in the right way, not as we should have, but there was support.

One of the things I didn't tell you was that I once taught a course on what happens in literature when the relationship between sisters is foregrounded. Seen like that, *Goblin Market*, a poem in which one sister is 'fallen' and the other isn't, reads quite differently. Then there are Cinderella's sisters, and the sisters in *Lear*. Which lot were we? The Brontë sisters working on their art? Mary and Martha? Which one was which? Perhaps we were Gorgons? Literature is littered with sisters, but they have to be looked at in the right way, through their own eyes and in relation to each other. Some of that won't be pretty, but at least our lives will be seen to matter. Of all these sisters I think you'd have understood the Bennett sisters best – their need to get married, their limited options. What am I doing, my patient one?

Why am I trying to give you a grounding in English Literature? Because I have no other language.

Even though I couldn't paint at all, I thought that your paintings didn't really matter. There. I've said it. I thought of your work as a hobby. That was not sisterly. But then you didn't think of my work at all. So there! No point in flinging charges at each other. Let us give each other the attention and respect we should have given earlier.

There were things I wanted to tell you. When you watched the gods on television or did puja at home, your belief in the gods was literal. Mine wasn't. Ai had made me promise that I would never stop searching for the face of god. I didn't understand what she meant, but I had promised. Eventually, for me, it meant trying to understand myth more and more deeply. It was a quest, not a settling down to a fixed set of beliefs. Trying to understand the meaning of metaphors is not irreligious, even if it is true that myths mutate and that metaphors have many meanings. If you had thought I was irreligious, would you have minded? I think you would have just included me in your blessing. Towards the end you had decided that I was more inclined to be a Buddhist than a Hindu and that was all right – the Buddha was also a god. It reminded me of the time two of the Cloudies brought home some holy pictures from their convent school and showed them to Ai. Everyone thought she would be cross, but she just stuck them with the other gods in the *dev-ghar.*

I once tried to tell you one of my fables in Marathi. I thought 'The Mouse and the Lion' was one of my best fables, and one that I would be able to translate easily. At the time you were recovering from an operation for breast cancer. I thought I was trying to entertain you. Perhaps I was just showing off. When I got to the punchline, you and the nurse looked baffled. Serves me right. I went about it the wrong way, at the wrong time. I was thinking about myself, not about you. Nevertheless, it is important, don't you see? We don't have to accept the notions of justice and fair play that are imposed on us. Here it is again. It's only short.

> **THE MOUSE AND THE LION**
> One day a lion caught a mouse. "Spare me," said the mouse. "I am so little and you are so big, but who knows? Perhaps some day I will be able to do you a favour." The lion thought this funny and let the mouse go. But a few days later the very same lion was caught in a net. After a while the mouse came along. "Help," called the lion. "Help, little mouse. Chew through these ropes. Remember, after all, that you owe me a favour." The mouse started chewing and then suddenly stopped. "Why have you stopped?" roared the lion. "Well, I just thought of something," said the little mouse. "You see, I think I have already done you a favour." "You haven't," roared the lion. "Yes, I have," said the mouse. "What?" roared the lion. "Well, you see," said the mouse, "I haven't killed you."

My excuse for a benign lack of interest in your painting was that I didn't know anything about painting. So what? I could have asked, tried to learn. I could have given you the same attention I wanted from you.

I'm particularly ashamed of one of my clumsier efforts at 'taking an interest in your work'. I looked at a cupboard filled with your sketches and suggested you throw away most of them. I am so sorry. I must have hurt you. My point was these were only drafts, and that you should only keep the final one. I was thinking of all the wastepaper baskets I had filled in order to come up with a few good lines. I saw it as a mark of devotion to my craft. I suppose I could have tried to do the babble and doodle inside my head and saved a few trees.

Another time I offered to buy some of your work and was taken aback by the price you set. When I protested, you replied that an artist should be paid for her work – exactly what I've tried to tell publishers. After all, were we not engaged in the same activity – producing piece after piece of uncommissioned work? A Cloudy Uncle had one of your paintings of Shri Ganesh placed in the palace. M said it should be given the title 'Avuncular Indulgence'.

Another of the Cloudy Figures asked you one day in a jocular fashion, "Which of you is better, the Painter or the Writer?" "We're equally good," you replied equably. What, I wondered, was the point of the question? Were they putting you down? Putting me down? Just making conversation? Were we expected to establish the value of our work? You didn't care. I cared a little. You were untrained, but you had a great many bird books and teach yourself books. I didn't realise at the time how good it was for me to see the sheer pleasure you took in paints, watercolours, oils, acrylics, pastels, crayons, pencils, sketch books, drawing paper, silk, cardboard and canvas board. I watched you absorbed in your painting, copying, tracing and colouring; and years later when people asked me why I wrote, I answered with the truth I had learnt from you – "I like doing it."

Each time I visited, you painted new pictures especially for me, mostly birds and one resplendent Ganesh. At the time I accepted them casually, gracelessly. I am looking at them properly now. One is of a pair of – green bee-eaters? – on a bough. The beak isn't right for bee-eaters. I should have asked you when I could have and made a note. You've traced or copied them onto off-white silk and coloured them in so carefully. You so delighted in their plumage. I can see your hand moving the paintbrush, your eyes intent on the colours you might use, and I am glad I have the memory and I grieve. The other picture is of a pair of parrots. The two pictures go together. You've signed them "Minu" and dated them carefully 14-7-2002. They're the same size, about 10" by 16". You've sealed the edges with green ribbon, and attached a string by which I can hang them. I do not need the pictures to remember you; and yet, they contain something of you and I will look at them again and again.

They're not bee-eaters, they're coppersmith barbets! I asked a friend to ask her friend, who is a birdwatcher, if he knew what they were. He said at once that they were coppersmith barbets and was pleased he could identify them. And my friend was pleased she could tell me who they were. I was pleased too. All that pleasure seemed to come from you from the distant past.

The picture of Ganesh you gave me is larger and more spectacular. It's done on canvas board and the back is dated April 1995. You've framed it for me and it's studded with little mirrors and glass jewels so that Shri Ganesh is suitably decked. I think he was your favourite god as he is mine. You've signed it "Bharati Namjoshi" as well as "Minu". It carries a double blessing, both from the god and from you. I should have realised that long ago. I am very stupid sometimes.

Suppose it was established incontrovertibly that in the eyes of the world our work was worthless, or the opposite – that we were both geniuses, what difference would it make? How would it matter? I think doing good work does matter, but is doing bad work culpable? I heard a writer assert this once. I replied, "I'm not much of a gardener, does that mean I'm not allowed to garden?" "Because thou art a virtuoso, shall there be no more cakes and ale?" I made that up – Sir Toby to Malvolio. Do you think it's quite witty? But I would not have told it to you – different languages. Now I can, when we are suddenly free to say what we like to each other – now that it's too late.

I'm not sure how to think about being stupid or clever – what does it mean? I've often thought that education does as much harm as good – all that conditioning. For example children sometimes stop being able to understand poems because they've learnt to use language analytically and descriptively. They think the paraphrase of a poem is the poem. There I go again.

I wrote fables about birds and beasts. You drew birds and landscapes and endless portraits of Shivaji Maharaj. Marathas do that even though it's always the same portrait, the same statue. One day I set a trap for you. I asked you, "Who do you think was greater, figures like the Buddha or like Jesus, or Shivaji Maharaj?" You answered so wisely, my darling. You looked at me with your candid eyes and said, "The Buddha and Jesus were gods, Shivaji Maharaj was a man." You understood more than I thought you did, more perhaps than I did, because you were straightforward, whereas I could get lost in a tangle of words.

> The last to desert will be words,
> scurrying away
> on tiny two legs, carrying
> with them
> parcels of memory, leaving me unable
> even to plead.

But I do not believe you will leave me. You are steadfast. At the very end you will take my hand and I will stop grieving. And the painting of Shri Ganesh that you gave me and those of birds, I will put them on my wall and look at them properly.

5

In the Garden Elsewhere

It seemed strange to me that you had been to places I never knew. I was arrogant, I should have listened more instead of always assuming I knew more, knew better. And when I did keep quiet and listen, I did so patronisingly. I went away and I returned, while you were always there. I thought I knew what your life was like. At the same time I was baffled. I knew I didn't know. How could I possibly know more about you than you know about yourself? And when I disappeared into the cold countries, where did you think I had gone? When there was some talk of M visiting me, one of her brothers teased her: "You will go to cold Canada and will be walking down the street chewing paan and tobacco. And when you spit absentmindedly, all the natives will cry, "Look, look! See, see! Indian princess spitting rubies!" All of us, all the Cloudy Figures, found this very funny. After all, we were not unaware of the ironies inherent in exoticism.

I missed you, and thought about you being here, in this garden, which I have tried to tend so carefully even though I was ignorant about gardening. I wanted to show you the birds – blue tits, blackbirds, robins – just ordinary birds. You would have liked them. I wrote about being in this garden, but I'm not sure who the speaker is – you or me?

> In the garden elsewhere
>
> they are tending roses.
>
> The leaves are turning.
>
> The leaves have fallen.
>
> They are sweeping up leaves.
>
> There are no more roses.
>
> They are still in their garden.
>
> The distances drift.

You must be the speaker thinking about being here because of the reference to leaves falling and having to be swept up. We talked about your coming to visit, but your health made it impossible. Your doctors said that the medical system here would overwhelm you, and, moreover, air travel wasn't good for you. And the insurance companies told me that they would not insure anyone for pre-existing conditions. What would I have done if you had needed to see doctors again and again? It would have bankrupted me. And be honest, you liked seeing doctors.

I should have tried to tell you more about my life, explained that there were no servants. I did tell you that, but I don't know how well you understood the implications for daily life. And I should have realised that just knowing where you lived and having some idea of your daily routine wasn't enough. I phoned frequently. You said you were well. I asked what you were doing. You said you were painting and drawing, or sometimes you said you were watching TV. I asked whom you had seen and you said that you had gone for a drive with a Cloudy Cousin, the one who was the same age as you, or that one of the others had dropped by or that you had seen this doctor or that. You asked how I was, and like you, I was always well. You asked after Gill, my partner, and those of my friends whose names you could remember. And I said they were all right, or had this problem or that.

And yet, I did not know the texture of your days or what you were feeling. Suppose we had told each other that we were lonely, that we were in trouble, or that we were not in trouble, that we were happy, depressed, anxious, what could we have done? What could we have shared? To reach across the ocean we would have needed unimaginably long extensions with a pair of waldos at the end, padded, clumsy, barely able to pick up anything.

You had been abroad. M had taken you to Denmark for the heart operation. You remembered as much as you could about it, the kindness of the people, the food, the hospital room; and then you flew back too tired to do any sightseeing. That you could have gone sightseeing after a heart operation is laughable, isn't it? An egregious question, but I think I asked about sightseeing, because at the time I hadn't gone abroad yet. It was only many years later that I went to Copenhagen as a tourist. I tried to find the hospital you had been in, but I'm not sure I found the right one.

If I had gone on at length about what life was like for me, added detail after detail, perhaps you'd have said:

> You live your complicated life
> in a far country
> which is not unreal. It is, with effort,
> reachable;
> but there are rivers to ford,
> oceans to cross,
> mountains to fly over, and a mind that says
> it is not possible.

The spaces in which we lived didn't stay the same. The years went by. We changed. Circumstances changed. I had given up my job in Canada and had very little money. Where you lived, the configurations of the Cloudy Figures altered, you were more circumscribed. I don't think either of us fully realised how each of us had been affected. Some changes happen so slowly, happen when we're not looking. Our understanding was limited, but we were loyal. Just to be with each other, to be in the same space from time to time, that was solace, a space within a space.

You never questioned me, my smoking and drinking, though I knew perfectly well you didn't approve. If you had scolded me, I would have explained that a drink now and then made the house in which you lived tolerable for me at least for a short time. And yet you lived in it without the aid of alcohol or tobacco. Were you superhuman then? So exceptionally sane that you could do without these weaknesses and still withstand the constant erosion of daily life?

There were abrasions, there was hurt, there was pain, there were disappointments, and in order to cope with them you sometimes behaved absurdly. If I now ask you about the strange things you did (while refraining from mentioning my own idiocies), it is only to try to understand what it was really like having to be you, to endure what you endured and to live the life you lived. Men sometimes put women on a pedestal, expect them to behave better than them, and all in the interests of a double standard. The Cloudy Figures tended to see you as The Innocent One. I colluded in this. It was convenient to think that you were incapable of any negative feelings. You were the one without guile, the one who could be cheated with impunity because you 'did not understand'. Isn't it possible that you did understand, but were helpless? And because you could do nothing, you kept silent and the pain manifested itself in absurdities?

What absurdities?

You challenge me. The hoarding for one thing. Old clothes, old shoes, all your old sketches. I am not lumping your sketches with old shoes, but shouldn't one clean out some things from time to time just in order to live? Even memory doesn't retain everything, otherwise how would we manage? Mostly it was the old newspapers and clippings that puzzled everyone. Were they a defence? Against what? I am being ingenuous now. If even the great Mr Eliot could talk about fragments he had shored, then why shouldn't you keep your scraps?

Lots of people are hoarders.

Of course they are. It's not your imperfections I'm pointing to, it's your humanity. But you're still on guard. "What else?" you say, tilting your chin. Your hypochondria. You loved seeing doctors. You made totally unnecessary appointments to see them as often as you possibly could. "And wouldn't you if you had all my medical problems? In addition to my heart problem, I have had a stroke, I have had cancer, and I have to take blood-thinning medicines. When I bleed, it's hard to staunch the flow. I needed to be attended to, and if I had to pay doctors, well then I paid them. What is the difference between a sick person and a hypochondriac?"

Some of the Cloudy Figures maintained that you actually liked being in hospital. You liked the attention and the fuss. I wonder. I think you just wanted to make sure from time to time that your health was being properly monitored. The Indian hospitals were all right, but not clean enough in my opinion. Food for you was always sent from home and you had your own nurses. M took you to Copenhagen for that major heart operation on the advice of a visiting British surgeon. Ai and I waylaid him at a Bombay hospital. We asked him whether it would be safer for you to have your operation abroad. He must have seen our anxiety and answered properly. He told us that there wouldn't be a difference in the operation itself, but that the aftercare was better abroad. You didn't show the slightest fear. That wasn't lack of understanding. That was resolution.

Have you anything else to add?

You sound almost icy. Don't be cross, my darling. If I talk about weaknesses, these are not accusations, these are the outward signs of underlying suffering which I ought not to have ignored.

Anything else?

The oscillations and vacillations. I'm mumbling, afraid I have gone too far.

When?

During the brief period when you were married. You wanted to be taken away from his wretched household. Someone went to bring you back. I went or a Cloudy Uncle went. When you returned, you showed me your hands – cracked and roughened. They had made you scour the cooking vessels with ashes. This was not unusual punishment, it was what they did, how they lived. But then you demanded to go back, then to return with your body bruised. This happened time and time again, until it finally stopped.

Was it so very wrong to want the ordinary things that most people have – a husband, children, an occupation, friends?

Of course it was not wrong. I went back and forth, back and forth, across the seas for I don't know how many years. Sometimes it's best to accept that one cannot have what one wants to have. In the end that's what you did, spoke placidly and cheerfully about your foray into marriage and your divorce. You had wanted a husband and insisted on it to such a degree that finally M bought you one. I wanted to protest, but you would have been angry, and who was I to say it would not work?

How else did I behave oddly?

The stealing. The petty pilfering once or twice when we were in school together briefly.

You ignored me. How else was I to draw attention to how unhappy I was?

I'm sorry. Then there was the time you took a pair of earrings to a jeweller to sell. He brought them back. They were your own, so it was hardly stealing. But what did you want the money for? I hope I didn't ask that. To be treated like a child and considered too 'innocent' to handle money responsibly couldn't have been fun.

It wasn't. Go on. Now that you've begun, you might as well finish the job. What else?

Your strange eating habits: wanting constant snacks, limes to suck, ordering the same dishes whenever we went to a Chinese restaurant – chicken fried rice and ginger chicken.

You're one to talk! Given a chance you'd live exclusively on meat and sugar! It's a miracle you were never sick.

Yes, all right. Idiosyncrasies are, shall we say, normal?

Who shall declare what is normal? Carry on. Any last questions?

Yes, one. Why didn't you get your teeth fixed?

When he tried to put the implants on top of the posts he had driven in, it hurt. How many times do I have to tell you that? Can't you understand what it feels like to be somebody else? Anything more?

Well, just one small thing – all the money you wasted buying useless stuff. Your shopping habits. Did spending money help at all?

Any money I wasted wasn't a hundredth of what you and the Cloudy Figures squandered. But you were 'normal' and I was 'handicapped.' You're waving the double standard!

I'm sorry. I'll drop the subject. I'll examine the beam in my own eye.

How will that help?

I just remembered. You nodded off sometimes for a few moments when we were playing cards.

So what?

It was because you stayed up half the night watching TV. The servants connived in it. It was their one source of entertainment.

That and us.

Do you think they found us entertaining?

I don't know. Now that I'm sufficiently stripped, what is your diagnosis, O Pseudo-therapist?

I wasn't trying to diagnose. I wanted us to talk honestly.

First learn to listen honestly.

I'm sorry. I've invaded your privacy without permission. Even if we had occupied adjoining rooms, I should have knocked.

Would you have knocked on my skull? What should we do? Crack our heads open? Why don't you make a true dream instead, speak of a happy time – how it might have been. Stop this painful mining for a truth. Whatever the truth is, I do not think it's a gold nugget.

6

Interlude

Shall we begin with a daydream located in a different country?

Why in a different country? In a dream anything is possible even here.

Very well, let's start with Paragon, a chap who loves you enough to be friends with me.

Stop mocking me. I could marry a bear as in the old story of Snow White and Rose Red. So could you. They turn out to be princes.

Do you think that means that in order to have a happy ending males have to undergo a major metamorphosis?

You don't think much of men, do you?

I think that the identities that are on offer to men need changing. I'll tell you a story.

> **THE PROBLEM OF MEN**
>
> Once upon a time, two sisters set out on a journey. The older sister said to the younger one, "Let us be fierce, ferocious and formidable just like men. That way no one will bother us. In fact, let us pretend to be men."
>
> "Not a good idea." The younger sister demurred. "If we pretend to be men, we'll be treated like men; get slapped

on the back, bashed and buffeted, made to drink a lot and tell dirty jokes."

"Not all men do that."

"No, but many do. Let us be women, admit we are weaker, ask for protection and defer to men."

"And if the men don't agree?"

"Turn to the women."

"And if the women cannot or will not help?"

"Divide the species into the Civil and Evil and fight a war."

"You're absurd!" said the older one.

"Well," replied the younger one, striding ahead, "Between the impossible and the unbearable, what choice is there?"

I don't think men are bad.

You don't think anyone is bad. Perhaps I agree with you, but it's not that. I think an imbalance of power is harmful, whether between the Eloi and the Morlocks or between men and women. And I agree with Swift that as a species we could do with considerable improvement.

Turn into horses?

No, but do you remember the King of Brodingnag's indictment after Gulliver tells him about gunpowder?

Too harsh.

And he didn't know about nuclear weapons or global warming.

What would he have said?

Might have recommended extermination. Or not bothered as we're doing it ourselves.

Be nice.

All right let's talk about a good man. Squire Allworthy?

That old?

Tom Jones then.

Well ...

You're hopelessly heterosexual!

Why are you picking suitors for me out of English novels?

They seem to suit.

Darcy then?

The proud Mr D would have no use for me. I would be an embarrassment.

Do I have to have the approval of my elder sister before I marry? Still, I wouldn't have anyone who didn't like you. I mean whom you didn't like.

I would have tried to indulge him, even if I thought he was a sexist pig. But there is a problem. I'll tell you a poem I wrote. In it, I'm the girl with the sad face – the Knight of the Doleful Countenance.

Am I in it? Which one am I?

You are my sister, obviously. Here's the poem.

> The girl with the sad face
>   sets forth gallantly
> with no esquire.
>   She meets a knight,
> dares him to fight.
>   He kills her on the spot.
> The lady of the knight
>   murmurs to the knight,
> "I'm sorry you slew her.
>   She was my sister."

I would always take your side against someone who was trying to kill you!

Even if I had picked the fight? Besides, what could you do?

No one is trying to kill you. How can you dislike someone just for being a man?

I dislike male privilege.

It's hard to give up privilege. We don't say we'll trade places with the servants. Don't be so judgemental.

I'll try.

Besides, in a dream I could have someone as clever and kind as you.

I have not always been kind. Shall we go back to Paragon?

All right.

You can shape him as you like. I will forgive him all his vanities and silliness.

Why does he have to be silly?

People are. They can't help it. Very well. A charming and amiable Mr Bingley then.

What about children?

Children definitely. A boy and a girl. I think I would make a superior aunt. Have the girl first so she won't get bossed.

Someone like you? Absolutely non-bossy!

Are you teasing me?

Yes!

Do you know, I think we're having a normal conversation. The kind that ordinary sisters have – about boys, who's suitable and who isn't.

I wouldn't know. Can I have a career?

Something to do with wild life?

An ornithologist?

Or an ecologist?

Or someone who understands genes and evolution and all that?

Something like that. You're not asking for very much. Only for the possible.

In this dream I have good health and I lead a normal life.

And everything else stays the same. In the dream you are beautiful as in real life. In the dream you are charming as in real life, but you have more control over your mischief and your smiles.

I don't know about beautiful and charming, but yes, I would have liked a normal life – done the things other people do. If I could have had just one small change – no hole in my heart – I would have been all right.

Don't be so sure. Life bashes us all.

What would you have liked?

Not to have been hated and despised.

You weren't hated.

No? Not to have been sneered at for not fitting in, for not being heterosexual.

To change the world is hard?

Yes.

But you tried?

Yes. Changing yourself is even harder. You couldn't do very much about ill health, but you did your best to accept it. I admired you for that. It must have been hard?

I had to be patient, let people tell me that they knew best. And I had to make sure I got looked after and be grateful for it.

I'm sorry.

It was necessary. What did you have to do?

Get kicked, get bashed – metaphorically. Suffer the usual things people have to suffer for one reason or another. The hard bit was remaining sane.

What happened to our happy dream?

It has to be shaped with our hands, with skill. I wrote a poem called 'The Sonneteers of No Consequence'. We could be those sonneteers, walk quietly in a remote orchard, do no harm, cause no disturbance, trouble no one, then perhaps we'd be all right.

> The sonneteers of no consequence do not touch
> the fruit as they walk among the apple trees.
> They allow their senses to take as much

> pleasure as they wish, or as little, and so appease
> their tired minds. They observe that the air
> makes columns of light in the spaces in between.
> And all remains intangible: what's there
> and not there, what's seen and not seen.
> A summons of the mind could quickly destroy
> their quiet calm, or a whim arouse
> the habit of speech, unwittingly alloy
> their cloistered privacy, as they browse
> like sheep, not sonneteers, and stroll at ease
> in the spaces between those apple trees.

Sheep? Have you turned us into sheep?

Why not? Browsing contentedly in a pastoral.

7

Eloi and Morlocks

That last time we were together, your nurse, who had been with you for some time, said suddenly that you were her god, and that by serving her patients, she was serving the gods. She was explaining how she saw her work and her duty. She was a good-hearted person and had grown fond of you. I noticed that in those last days, some of the servants were very kind to you. For instance, they brought you whatever food you thought you could eat – fish, brownies, chips, soup, chicken, rice, anything. Then we stood around persuading you to eat it and you could not. It was heartbreaking and different from the old days when you asked for a snack every few minutes. Well, I'm exaggerating. But in those last days many of the servants were more than generous – they were loving.

Perhaps it would make equally good sense to say that they are gods – those who serve us. The rest of us are dependent on them. I wrote a poem about it once, a half joking 'Ode to Alexa,' the Amazon AI.

The small gods run about
like children
at night or like the toys of small children.
They're supposed
to protect us, so that all goes well
and nothing
is amiss. But if the gods have a duty,
then servants
are gods, so are AIs.
We got it wrong.
No bargain was ever made.
There was only our need.

Sometimes it seemed to me that our relationship to servants was like that of the delicate and useless Eloi to the hard-working Morlocks, who lived underground, while the flower-like Eloi floated above. Some of the servants were sometimes kind to us, even though we were crass – crass because we ignored how poor they were relative to us. You were stupid about them once – you called them 'stupid', but only once. You were aware of your dependence on them and far more grateful than most people. You knew that those who were kind to you deserved to be respected, and you gave them that respect, and even affection. This was not quite in keeping with what was considered the proper distance between classes. Perhaps, in a rigid society, we, who do not fit in, can see our kinship more easily to those for whom mobility is almost impossible – according to the Gliders.

Gliders? Just another name for the Cloudy Figures – the Gliders and the Floaters, those whose feet barely touched the ground, Eloi, as opposed to Morlocks. The latter played their part, one or two cheated you, one or two frightened you; mostly they served you and waited and watched. In Wells' vision of the future, the Eloi sometimes got eaten by the Morlocks.

Even Jane Austen's society has sometimes been described as a genteel jungle.

In our hearts I don't think either of us felt we belonged with the Eloi properly; but we also knew that if we suddenly had to live as Morlocks, we wouldn't survive. I wonder what the Morlocks thought of us – of the two Eloi sisters, playing cards, eating, sleeping, doing nothing useful?

The times changed and that affected everyone. The older servants, who had fitted into the feudal system, saw themselves differently. Some were even proud of their roles – the royal chefs – one Western, one Indian, the chap who tied Baba's turbans, the descendant of the mahouts who looked after us (a come down from elephants). They died one by one. The later generation were doing their jobs because they were jobs; they had some hope of getting on. There was the woman with HIV and a glorious smile. Did she know how ill she was? She had such a delight in being alive that just seeing her lifted one's spirits. She was let go. But the cook, who was unpleasant to everyone with such abandon that few could like her, was kept on. It was felt she was unlikely to leave, because no one else would take her on. After M's death she began terrorising you, and was let go. Then there was the clever and good-hearted driver, who always cheered you and was therefore forgiven any possible cheating. He brightened your days but when you could no longer go for drives, he too lost his job. In your will you rewarded them. I wonder what they made of it? Might they have thought that any reward was insufficient? I certainly thought so when I did odd jobs as a student in North America to keep myself going. The meat in the supermarkets at so many cents an ounce made me think that that was how I was selling my life – at so much an hour.

We were not unkind, but we colluded in the system and did our best to keep proper distance. We knew instinctively that not to do so would be a mistake. For everyone to know their place was convenient and sensible, and then we didn't have to think about the cruelty of it. And I call myself a feminist! What would you have said if I had tried explaining feminism to you? Perhaps you would have kept quiet and refrained from saying that beggars can't be choosers.

As Eloi are we entitled to talk about our sufferings, or even about our own experience? I did not love the Morlocks – with some exceptions. Nor did I love the Eloi – again with exceptions. In theory I despised the Eloi. Should we then despise ourselves? You didn't go in for despising people. What was it about your gaze? Was it kind? Benign? Clear-sighted like the eyes of young children? There's that phrase in Shakespeare – "The young-eyed cherubim." Are the cherubim ignorant or innocent? What do they know of human life?

There's basic selfishness. We each of us love ourselves best. You wanted to be looked after, to survive, no matter what that did to anyone else. I wanted my own life and never mind everyone else. Having admitted that, shall we shake hands?

Did you realise that the Morlocks also served another function? They were an audience, though not necessarily individualised, and their opinion was not required of them. All that was required was that they play their part, be suitably admiring, even obsequious. That would mean that the Gliders were always on stage – always aware of how they looked. No wonder it was so restful to get away, to walk by ourselves in the university gardens.

If we were on stage, we should consider how the others regarded us. The servants were the watchers watching us watch one another in the drawing room drama. I noticed that some of the Gliders talked to me rather than to you even though they had come to visit you because you weren't well. Did I take up all the oxygen in the room, even though you needed it more? Or, in other ways, did you, because you needed it?

I will tell you a truth I have discovered in the course of a fairly long life. People tend to like you or dislike you in accordance with whether they like or dislike themselves in your presence. That is why flattery works. People genuinely liked you. You didn't flatter them; I think it was because you liked them. As for me? I don't dislike people, I am a little afraid of them. On the whole I wish them well.

I expect the servants knew that people who were in love with their own image could be manipulated. It merely had to be insinuated that such and such an action was or wasn't in keeping with their image ...

Your ego, my darling, where was it located? It took me a long time to understand that a sin against my ego was not really important. You understood that from the beginning, despite growing up in a Maratha household in which self image, pride and honour mattered and any insult to the ego had to be instantly avenged. Had you given up on ego? When you forgave people so easily, it did not come across as gutlessness or a lack of pride, but as something beyond such considerations.

As for my image, it was only a conversation between me and my mirror. The people on whom I was projecting my image were often too absorbed in looking into their own mirrors to pay much attention. A Drawing Room Drama in which none of the actors were in the same play? But sometimes we used each other's eyes for mirrors. It's a dangerous game. People have to be careful.

A long time ago I wrote two or three scrappy lines. I wasn't sure what they meant. I understand them now.

> O mirror-eyed Medusa,
>   blind and mirror-eyed,
> take off your mask. My image
>   is fixed in granite now.

Perhaps we are all afraid, though we live in time and keep changing. There are many perceptions. Sometimes we try to turn each other into granite – Morlocks and Eloi alike – out of spite, out of convenience, out of laziness. Don't let this memoir catch you. It hasn't 'caught' you. With any luck we're two voices singing, laughing, talking – I hope some of your voice comes through – in the dark and in the daylight as the days slip by.

And we may not be just the Eloi Sisters. We are Morlocks as well – if not in strength, then in having been scarred and belittled – in some way perhaps everyone is. I think I realised this when I claimed kinship with the disabled. A group of them had been kind to me and so I dared to write this poem – about Morlocks = Eloi = Gliders = Subterranean Ones = Dwarfs = Snow White = Bears? Anyway, here's the poem.

THE DWARFS

Disabled doesn't mean disqualified,
or perhaps it does?

i)
Snow White sleeps
and the dwarfs go crazy, scrabbling
in the darkness
for the means of life.
They cannot covet her.
(It is not permitted.)
But possibly they love her.
What can she offer?

Possibly her presence,

perfuming their days

with light and love?

Look, but don't touch!

Wistful children
                    peer through the pane.
Who is their keeper?
                    And what the secret?
When Snow White wakes,
            who smashes open
                    their house of glass?

ii)
Later, no bitter lies, though dwarfs
may offer a silent surprise.
My name was Cordelia,
Though the mirror erased me,
my mother loved me
when I was very small.

iii)
My name was Stout Heart!
                    Mine Courage!
But our third sister
            —no, do not laugh—
she was the bravest of us all.
The bad queen thought her ugly.
The good queen thought her mad.
                    But the mirror
stopped its smirking,
                    grew thoughtful and sad.

iv)
Yes, I was bashful—
not first in the scuffle,
not first in the race—
both Backward and Bashful.

How explain?
I felt no lack, no loss of grace.

v)
And I wasn't sleepy, I was asleep.
My brothers didn't mind.
My sisters tended me.
When I woke up I told my dream.
They cried: Manna! Roses!
Lilies! Ice-cream!
Whatever was
or might have been.

vi)
Last but not least, I was beautiful.
Oh do not smile a reticent smile.
My name was Snow White, Sister, Dwarf.
Now no bitterness, no needless guile.

8

Someone Has to Get Eaten

I never tried to explain feminism to you. Because I thought you wouldn't understand? Because I didn't want to put an additional burden on you by having you question the status quo? I'm not sure why, but I want to try now. Here's a proposition: we are women and we matter.

I knew that.

In a patriarchy men rule and women come second. That isn't fair.

Men are bigger and stronger. They may not be better, but they do things and have most of the power. Like me you're a woman so I'm not wary of you and I'm not in awe of you. We're harmless. Well, not always.

Does one have to be frightened to respect someone? Might isn't right. I tried to explain to M once that women were oppressed because of the imbalance of power. She declared that she was certainly not going to see herself as an oppressed woman.

What's wrong with that? I don't think I'm downtrodden. It's not a good self-image.

Not everyone is privileged! To be oppressed isn't shameful. Doing the oppressing is.

That's not how people see it. You sound cross?

I want you to agree with me.

Why?

All right, don't agree. But don't you want to fight for your fellow women?

I don't want to fight at all. Have you ever tried picking up a sword? They're heavy. I don't think even you could wield one.

Look, being for women, doesn't mean being against men.

Yes, it does. You want to deprive them of all their privileges. Nobody likes that. Besides, men protect us.

Against whom do they protect us?

Other men.

Got you! Don't you see what that means?

It means that as long as men exist we need protection.

It's hopeless trying to convert you.

I'll make a deal with you. Convert the men first. And when they're all feminists, I'll become one!

Coward!

Not a coward. Just a realist.

I dedicated *Feminist Fables* to you in part. I said you were innocent and did not understand.

Why dedicate a book to me and then say I wouldn't understand it?

I'm sorry. Truly. But do try to understand what I'm saying. In a patriarchy we are second-class citizens. Let me tell you a story.

Another feminist fable?

Yes.

Go on then.

It's called 'The Cage'.

The tiger or the lady - well-thumbed images of fear and desire, but for whose consumption? He's a big game hunter, and has killed many ladies. It is what he does. It makes him feel good, adventurous and strong. It rouses his valour. The lady killing is pleasant sport, but the tiger, the burning and the brightness, that gets kudos. He aims between the eyes. Pop goes the gun! He has bagged his beast! That'll show his mates he's man enough.

To those of us who are not men - not that sort anyway - such pastimes might appear puerile, were they not lethal. We had best choose a different paradigm: one cage for the mighty hunters; and for the rest of us, none at all.

Don't you see what happens in a patriarchy?

I do see. But don't you see that I don't want to be thrown in the tiger's cage!

So you're willing to live in a cage of your own?

I know my limits and do what I can to look after myself. Are you a socialist as well as a feminist?

Yes.

Then why haven't you given your money to the poor?

I will when the time comes.

Me too. When the time comes I'll be a good feminist. Meanwhile, why don't you concentrate on being a good Hindu?

Why? I was born a Hindu.

Exactly. You shouldn't eat beef.

I shouldn't eat anyone. What else?

And you should light some incense for the household gods.

Once in a while I do light incense. I'm fond of the small gods. Does that make me a good Hindu?

I think everyone should be a good Hindu.

Why?

Then the world would be a happier place.

Wouldn't the world be equally happy if everyone were a good Muslim or a good Christian?

Not as happy. Besides I don't want to be a Christian or a Muslim.

But you want them to be Hindus?

No, that's up to them. Stop trying to trap me with words!

I think one of our ancestors got converted to Islam because he fell in love and then got converted back by Shivaji Maharaj. Which attitude do you think is more smug – wanting to convert everyone, or declaring that you're not interested in converting other people?

I would let 'them' decide – as opposed to 'us'. You're trying to trick me into saying something I don't want to say.

I'm sorry.

I don't dislike Muslims and Christians. Do you dislike people who are not feminists?

Only when they are horrible. All right, I'll be quiet and you tell me how you would make a better world.

It would be a paradise for birds.

Don't you like humans?

People are all right, but birds are prettier. We would be able to speak their language. We would twitter and cheep with the best of them. There would be no bullying, no cheating, no war. We would just enjoy looking at them and listening to them – albatrosses swooping and gliding on the wing, the courtship of cranes, and, of course, concerts. The shooting of birds would be totally banned. Also, the eating of eggs.

By whose order?

Mine. I would protect them. Just as the Queen of England protected swans.

She wasn't just the Queen of England, she was the queen of a whole load of other places.

So much the better for swans!

And she didn't protect swans. Only she was allowed to eat them.

Well, that's some protection.

You sound like Lord Gonzalo in *The Tempest* – "all men idle, all, / And women too, but innocent and pure."

Last time you said I sounded like Miranda. Who do you sound like?

I'm half-Caliban and half-Prospero, a cross between a fool and a would-be wise man. What would the raptors do in your bird paradise – the kites, the falcons, the eagles and the hawks?

They could eat mice.

You don't care about mice?

Someone has to get eaten. But if we're making this up, they could be vegetarian. So could the tiger in that fable of yours. The men would throw away their guns. I would re-write your fable so that no one would have to live in a cage. We would all live happily together.

You wish!

I do wish. So do you.

And you've taken to re-writing my fables?

Why not? In Grimms' Snow White and Rose Red *the bear eventually turns into a prince and Snow White marries him.*

And what about Rose Red?

She marries the prince's brother.

And you call that a happy ending?

All right, she marries the prince's sister.

I'm ambivalent about princes and princesses.

Why?

Because of all the people who are not-princes and not-princesses.

I would change the story so that anyone could be someone – girls, boys, bears, dwarfs ...

That's all very well, but do you realise that in a utopia of other people's making we might not qualify as citizens. In a good society there would have to be good people.

We're quite good.

But not good enough. Hitler, for instance, would have given us black triangles and done away with us.

Nobody thinks Hitler was good – not any more.

I wouldn't be allowed in a utopian society. And you wouldn't be allowed to be yourself. You'd have to be cured.

I don't mind being cured. Why wouldn't you be allowed? Because you're a lesbian?

No, because I'm a fabulist and a poet.

Poems and fables are ok. Utopians like them. They think they are harmless.

No they don't. A utopian society is very nearly perfect. Questioning it would amount to a crime.

Why would you want to change it if it was feminist and socialist and all that?

Because we live in change. Anything that's static kills what's alive. Poets and artists are constantly reshaping. Shelley got it wrong. We are not legislators. And the patterns we make are not fixed in time. They contain time.

What are you then?

Gadflies! Like Socrates.

So you're a subversive going against law and order?

Exactly. In most societies that's considered a crime.

Well, I would help you.

Then you'd be in trouble.

We'd hide underground – like the Morlocks.

We're less powerful and more troublesome than them. We could pretend we were someone else.

Is that what people do?

Yes.

If a perfect society isn't for ordinary people, how may we live?

With awareness.

Of what?

Of our imperfections.

All these words to arrive at that? I could have told you that right at the start. You're just an idealist.

And you're a realist?

Of course. I had to be just to survive.

9

She Was a Good Egg

We could be swans floating side by side down the river.

Which river? Swans are rare visitors here.

This river here, only three miles from where I live. There are lots of swans.

Now that I'm gone we could pretend to be anything, float anywhere. You imagine things. You don't know what it was really like.

Tell me then.

I was born on the 19th of January 1945 in the city of Bombay in a private hospital on Marine Drive. We were still part of the British Empire. Bombay – Mumbai now – was never a cold place, but I was cold and found it hard getting born. I was a blue baby – not enough oxygen, but I stayed alive. I don't remember much of those early years. I had siblings a little younger than me. They were all right. And I had an older sister. She was more difficult. She didn't pay enough attention to me. She was busy doing her own things – mostly reading books – when she should have been talking with me or playing with me. She did talk sometimes, threw off remarks in a misleading manner. And when we played she was always boss. For instance she was Captain Marvel to my Mary Marvel, or Superman to my nothing –

Stop it. This is embarrassing!

You embarrassed me!

I was trying to show that you were human, not some innocent angel suffering in silence, that you made an effort and lived your life well.

Exactly. You are human too. This older sister, when she was doing her own thing or being boss, demanded certain privileges by virtue of being older than the rest of us. She would go out with our parents sometimes, while we stayed at home. It wasn't fair. And she had a room of her own when we were in Bangalore. It was only a bit of the veranda partitioned off. We managed to throw straw into it over the partition just to annoy her. The point is she thought she was very important. She was important to me, but not as important as she thought she was. What she never realised was that the most important thing about her was that she was hardly ever there – an Important Absence. Just like Dad after he was killed in his plane crash. Anyway, this older sister went to boarding school, then to university and then she went abroad and flew in now and then like a stray pigeon. M and the Cloudy Figures were at least present. I could talk about them, but this is her book and she says it's to be about us. What am I supposed to say?

I could talk about the things that never happened. I never left home. I did not go to university. I did not earn a living. I did not have children. Should I add that I was not respected, that I was not loved? That would not be true. Some of the Cloudy Figures held me dear. As for my sister, who likes to call herself Rose Green, now that I am gone, she is devastated, as though she has lost half herself. It's strange, isn't it, that we are closer now after my death, than we were before and say things we never said. Of course I loved her and still do, but in case she gets too complacent, I'll tease her with a cliché from the country she lives in: "She was a good egg."

And that's my epitaph? You're making me wince.

Serves you right. It's what younger sisters do.

Why?

It evens things up.

We're not fighting.

I had an ego too. Lived in my own light, not in your shadow.

Of course. But I don't want to be called a 'pigeon'. I called you a 'swallow'.

All right, you can be a swallow too. Tell me something you didn't tell me when you could have.

I wished I was as good looking as you and my features were as fine.

I knew that! Something else.

I wanted you to admire me for being a good writer.

Really? You respected my judgement? Wasn't it enough that I loved you?

That was everything. You know that. It made me feel I was fortunate – loved by the gods.

Go on. Another confession.

You want to draw blood?

Why not? As you said, it will prove that you are human.

I envied you your dimples.

Why didn't you tell me that? I would have felt good knowing that there was something about me you envied. Tell me one more thing.

Dogs. I envied you your power over dogs. What did you do or say to ferocious dogs that turned them gentle?

That's easy – I liked them. But that's not just telling. That's asking. I'll ask you a question. What are you really trying to do?

I'm trying to find you.

How? By looking under the bed? Searching behind the bushes? We are not children, playing hide and seek. Besides, I was always there in plain view. You disappeared.

I know.

Why don't you tell the truth? You think by writing about me you'll immortalise me.

If the casual, implacable insolence of death could be answered by building a monument or by writing an elegy, perhaps it would do till language crumbled and the edifice fell. And yet I do want you to be remembered. The world sometimes thinks that people like you are a burden and that people like me are a bloody nuisance. It is not so. What you gave the world was a balm, needed for healing. And what I gave was my best work, which I hoped would also heal. I want people to know that you mattered, that you had something to give the world that was worth having. But I don't think that's the main reason I'm writing this. I miss you!

I understand. When I was very little I thought you were much bigger and stronger than me. You never were really, were you? Y ou needed looking after. I tried.

Yes, you did. It made a difference. There must be another garden where we can walk together again. I don't mean the Elysian Fields covered in asphodel. Out of memory we can construct another garden, or make a better one, even a better world.

We tried that. You wanted to know what the birds of prey would do in my bird paradise – what they would live on. Don't invent things. Try to remember how things were.

I can only remember what I do remember. How can I know what I didn't know? I can dredge memory and spread what I find before you. For instance, you liked the colour pink. When I bought a white bed sheet instead of a pink one because it was a better buy, you were cross with me. "I like what I like," you informed me. You were right, of course.

You drank cod liver oil occasionally when you were little. Actually put the bottle to your mouth and glugged it down. Did you need it, I wonder?

I nearly got us both killed by trying to cross an intersection with great confidence. We were only little.

You drank some iodine or they thought you might have drunk some. Dad held you upside down. Nothing happened.

When we were all children you fooled a little Cloudy into eating a piece of soap. Told him it was cheese. I don't know whether this is apocryphal.

Once when a thief entered the house, you were so indignant that you shouted at him and he ran away, which was lucky.

When we were at that American school, you and I had a screaming contest on the merry-go-round. You won hands down.

You kept a pair of baby chipmunks called Chip and Munk till one of them bit you.

You wouldn't let me listen in peace to the Radio Ceylon Superman slot even though you couldn't understand a word of it.

I gave you a brown opal, which I had brought back from Australia. Had it made into a ring. You didn't like it and gave it back to me and then asked for it again. Admittedly, a prettier opal would have been better. I suspect you thought it looked like a cockroach. It did a bit.

When I asked why you were feeding the birds on junk food – *bhel* of all things, you replied, "Because they like it and so do I."

You asked me for a bird feeder or perhaps you didn't ask, but I brought it anyway. Your birds wouldn't eat from it. They thought it was outlandish. The birds here in this English garden won't eat rice. They think it's exotic.

Did you know that I sometimes cheated when we played cards – not often – and let you win? Sometimes you kept winning even when I wasn't trying to lose and then I was chagrined! Serves me right.

One day you pinched my riding boots. I was startled. I didn't mind. When was I ever going to use them again? Were there some things I did or had done that you hankered to do as well?

Every now and then you claimed that one or another of the Cloudy Figures had a special fondness for you. Who doesn't want to be loved? You never asserted that I cared about you. You didn't need to.

Do you remember asking me to bring back bird books and books for drawing? And being pleased when I got the right ones, and cross when I didn't?

Do you remember the time I said to you, "Call your driver and get me out of here. We have to go for a drive." You didn't argue. I had just had teeth out and didn't want to be humiliated. I couldn't bear to be with anyone except you.

You loved listening to Hindi film music. You played it loudly on your transistor while I was trying to study. I learnt to delete it from my sensory input. Sounds good doesn't it – sensory input?

And do you remember the teachers in that first boarding school gathered about as you howled and screamed? They didn't know what to do. They summoned me, but I didn't know what to do either. I should have comforted you.

Do you remember the Himalayan black bears in the Lucknow zoo? We'd throw peanuts at them and they'd catch them in their mouths.

The magpie robin on the edge of the bird bath you had set up, jumping in and splashing about? The peacocks we saw sometimes when we drove to the right place? The kingfishers? And the kites soaring on rising thermals?

In Bumbroli, we'd cross the train tracks and sit on the tarmac of the small aerodrome and watch the planes land – tiny two-seaters, piper cubs and tiger moths. You played with a large worm there once which turned out to be a baby snake, though I'm not altogether sure that's true.

And you fell over and banged your forehead on the edge of a thali. You had the scar for years. You were a baby and I must have been quite little, but I think I remember it.

Different things happened in different places – Allahabad, Mussoorie, Lucknow, Phaltan, Pune, Mumbai, Bangalore. Even Delhi, though I can't remember anything that happened there in which you were involved. Perhaps you weren't born yet?

And these bits and pieces are not chronological. How can they be? In the sea of memory everything is simultaneous; every now and then a fish leaps. This is better in a way than ordinary interaction. Does it help? It helps me, keeps you from drifting further and further away.

I want to tell you about a dream. A dream is not factual, but it's not invention. I really did dream this the other night. You and I were playing cards and we decided to use food for money. I don't know whether we ever really did that. Perhaps we used til-gul for money. Or peppermints. Or chocolates. In the dream, my share of food-money contained a pig. I thought that was good until the pig started eating up the rest of my food-share. I told you about it and you laughed. It felt good to see you laugh.

10

Elephant

We've talked about things that happened and didn't happen, but we've left out the elephant in the room, although I don't think she would like to be called Elephant. I mean Mother, to whom I've referred ever so coyly as M. Many years after I went to live in the West, I consulted a respected psychoanalyst. We only had one session, but the first thing she said was, as though stating the obvious, "Ah, the problem is mother." I wonder if that would have been true of you. You were, as you saw it, wholly dependent on her. And you were steely about it. You had to survive. In your eyes the main function of anyone was how useful she or he was in looking after you. And so you didn't judge her. No, I'm not sure that's true. I think perhaps you genuinely loved her and respected her. She looked after you and she did it from the day you were born to the day of her death. She died three years before you. Who can blame her if she was weary – and sorry for herself? I can, though I'm not sure it's a sensible way to think.

I said to her once, "Why are you unhappy? Things aren't too bad. Your children are all right," to which she replied, "What's that to me?" She had a point. Children are often self-centred. They forget that parents are human beings, have their own lives.

She told me about a dream in which there was a great feast at which there were many people. Everyone had a silver thali laden with good things. But her plate was empty. I didn't know what to say to that.

Perhaps she was remembering her parents' table from the old days; even I remember it from when I was little. Everyone had a great silver platter, little silver ramekins for various dishes, and a silver glass for water. The salt and the slice of lime were at the top, miscellaneous things like pickles and chutneys were on the left, the more substantial dishes on the right, rice and chapatis at the bottom. Sometimes I had to sit with the grown-ups, eat properly with my right hand, and wait till everyone had finished eating. Later the silverware was divided among the children. I think M sold her share to help pay the school fees. I suppose if you're a princess and life hasn't treated you the way you would have liked, you are more outraged than most people. I should have consoled her as I would have consoled a friend – by agreeing that things had been hard and then praising her for her strength. But mothers aren't friends. Perhaps they should be. Was she your friend?

I wanted her approval. I tried for many years and failed. It was only after her death and after I read her will that I gave up trying. She told me once that she had dreamt about me. In this dream there was an apple tree. Half its apples were golden and beautiful, but the other half were poisonous. I suppose she was referring to my homosexuality. Was she genuinely homophobic or did she just hate the social implications? But she was wrong. I was foolish and failed often, but there was no poison in me. Had Dad lived, he would have told her so. He too was capable of making mistakes, but in this he would not have been wrong.

I accepted that she was homophobic. I accepted also that she only wanted to give us – that is you and me – a life interest in her house. I forgave her that as well. After all, houses, money, all these are metaphors for feelings. And I wanted to be at peace with her before she died. But to have left us without even that? During her last days I was kind and affectionate. You were not. I think you were startled that at last her health was more fragile than yours. I do not think how we behaved mattered to her any more. Perhaps she was still busy looking in the mirror, or perhaps by then she was beyond that.

I now understand the function of the mirror and why the queen kept looking into it. She was examining her image, and wanted reassurance that she was the noblest of them all. I found a photograph on which M had written on the back: "This is the last day that I can call myself a princess." I suppose marrying Dad was a grand sacrifice. When she disinherited us, did she think she was founding a dynasty? She saw herself as a noble person, who had suffered much, and had endured it all for a very long time. It's true that she had suffered and endured. And was noble because she had been born a princess? She read out a poem to me once that she had written in Marathi, 'Mi Pashan' – 'I am stone'. It seemed to be saying that though everyone else was allowed to have feelings, she wasn't. Her destiny was to be stone, to pretend she felt nothing, no matter how great her suffering. How could we appease such dearth, such desolate need?

It's strange how different elements in the Snow White story enter this account. Many years ago I wrote a prose poem called 'Glass Coffins'. I was thinking about Dad and about losing him.

> There were two glass coffins, the prince was in one and Snow White in the other, and though the sun glared and the leaves fell, the glass was undamaged. They were like pretty marionettes in cellophane wrappers waiting to live. And the dwarfs were not miners, they were cybernetic experts, wise wiremen doing their damnedest to trigger the dream. Then a thought leaped an arc. A sudden impulse:

"Cough up that apple." Snow White coughs. "Break through the glass." Her fist crashes. The dream begins. Stepping so gingerly, so timidly on grass she approaches the prince. He has snow-white hair. This is no prince. This is the king. He died in his sleep. She buries him. Then "Cough up that apple." Snow White coughs. "Break through the glass." Had she time to consider, she might prefer not to dream.

We were all affected by his death, traumatized even. Perhaps I missed him more because I was the eldest, had known him longer. In the dream in which he was back again, there were variations on the plot. Waking up hurt. You wanted me to tell you everything I could about him. What could I tell you? That he was fallible and he was kind. And I was not afraid of him. My greatest charge against him was that he died.

I can understand Mother disinheriting me. I was a disgrace; I had gone away; I had not stayed in the closet and so had besmirched the family name. I can understand, but not agree. But why did she disinherit someone as helpless and innocent as you? How were you culpable? You survived. That you would do so easily wasn't clear at the time she secretly revised her will. Money matters in itself even though the whole system is unjust. What matters even more is that the will was an expression of her feelings. She was in her nineties, didn't know what she was doing? Perhaps. The Cloudy Figures rallied around. You were looked after. By then there was enough money.

As you see, I'm much exercised by who she was and what she did. You and I never discussed her. The two of you were a dyad, had lived together for such a long time. Of me she said that after I had ceased to be a very small child, she and I had never been together for more than three months at a time. As I was leaving, you made me kiss her photograph respectfully. I did so to placate you. What were you trying to tell me? Did you suspect my ambivalence? Did you forgive her? Or did you think there was nothing to forgive? You knew her better than anyone else. Perhaps you are right. The best that I can say of her was that she was human and shaped by circumstances she could not control. When you and I kissed each other good night, she would look at us sardonically. We ignored that; we knew that gentleness was good for us. She did not wreck our affection for each other. I don't think it mattered to her. I wonder if what went wrong was that she did not feel loved, and what we had to offer was not enough?

As an experiment to see if she would like it – this was naughty of me – I copied out Emily Dickinson's poem for her: "The Heart asks Pleasure—first— / And then—Excuse from Pain—" She loved it. What keeps that poem from being sentimental? Sheer skill? The fact that it's in the third person and therefore a general statement about the human condition?

I can see you beginning to shake your head at me. You want me to think something else, to feel something else. All right, let's talk about ourselves. Try this version of the old story.

> Once upon a time there were two sisters called Snow White and Rose Red who loved one another. They laughed and played all day long. And at nightfall Rose Red tucked her sister into bed. She said, "Good Night," also "Farewell."
>
> "You'll come back, won't you?" asked Snow White.
>
> "Yes," replied Rose Red, knowing as she did so, that this was a promise that would be kept.

You still shake your head. What can I say that will appease you? Then I realise that I am looking for something that will appease me. You were always so gallant. I'm the one that's wailing. Towards the end when I phoned you from England, you would say to me firmly, "Don't worry about anything. I am absolutely all right." It was absurd. Were you convinced that you had managed to convince me?

Here's a last poem, no, I'll turn it into prose. No, not even a prose poem. I'll just tell it to you. When we were children and had six sweets, we'd share them fairly; or if we had six eggs, we'd break them open, make an omelette, and eat half each. But now, day breaks and you do not share it; and I'm made less hungry for more eggs, more sweets ...

You still look at me sadly out of dark eyes as though I haven't got it quite right. Those last days, my darling, when we pleaded with you to eat and you did your best if only to please us, though in our hearts we all of us knew that there wasn't much point – how shall I learn patience from you and forbearance?

"You stole my peppermints," you point out slyly, trying to lighten things.

"Yes, I did," I reply unashamed. I wish we still had the peppermints. I wish I could still steal them. I cannot tell you that the day breaks and as I step outside my room at the meditation centre, I nearly stumble over a robin. It was hoping for crumbs. You'd have wanted to know, but you aren't listening. And I can see a purple sky, brushed with pink underneath; you cannot see it. Another last poem.

> The wind has forsaken you.
> The sun has turned dark.
> And the birds to whom
> you were always faithful
> say nothing at all.
> One by one he took
> away your senses.
> Was that how it was?

I've given myself ten good years starting from the beginning of this year. And now I have 3619 days left. Not a large number. I could probably count up to that number if I put my mind to it. I'm running fast like a runner on a treadmill. It's silly. I'll get there anyway. Don't misunderstand. I'm not depressed. I want to make the most of each day, of what is on offer, however limited – as you did! It's my turn to copy you. But I miss you. A world without you makes me uneasy, it's lacking. Do you remember once, just once, in the middle of telling me how you were perfectly all right, you told me how much you missed M and me. I'm sorry, my darling. If things had been different ...

I offer to write a history of who we never were and what we never did, to which you reply, "How could we have been different if the world wasn't different?"

When I don't say anything, you ask, "Why are you sad?" You decide to tell me a story:

> Once upon a time there were two sisters who loved one another.
>
> One day, Rose Green asked Snow White, "Would you give up your life for me?"
>
> "I'm not sure. I don't think so," replied Snow White.
>
> "That's sensible," answered Rose Green. "Let's enjoy what we've been given and live out our lives." And so they did for quite a long time.

"Are you appeased?" you ask.

I nod. "And M? Is she appeased? She looked after you for nearly three quarters of a century. I do not think I could have done it."

This makes you smile. For you there is never anything to forgive. Because of you, I stray unwittingly into your climate of generosity and love.

And while that's true, I've just realised that I have been stupid

– yet again. I've assumed that your gentleness, your kindness that I loved so much, was some sort of grace you had, a gift from heaven. I should have understood that it was *earned*. Like anyone else, you wanted a full and happy life, but you were limited and had to accept your limitations, had to accept that the marriage didn't work out, that there were things you couldn't have. No one finds such acceptance easy. That requires huge and constant effort – and wisdom.

I've said to you that the world you lived in was toxic for me. I should have understood more clearly that it was not easy for you to live in either. In our own way each of us was made aware that we were imperfect daughters, not quite what was desired. I escaped. You had to live in that milieu and fight for your existence every day without becoming a doormat. Sometimes you dealt with it by being obstinate and sometimes by retreating into painting pictures. It couldn't have been easy to remain generous. There was a time when you became more and more depressed. M bought you a motor car and provided a driver. Being able to go out on drives helped. Perhaps it offered spaces outside the set of the drawing room drama? For me, being with you was what made the discomfort of coming 'home' tolerable. I didn't see clearly that not being alone didn't mean that you were not lonely, that you waited for me to come for sheer companionship, and not just because you wanted to see me.

Do you remember a glorious few days we spent together at the home of a Cloudy Cousin in the country? He provided a car and a driver for us day after day and we went to the different reservoirs and dams nearby and looked at the flamingos and the storks and the cranes and the ducks; and that was when the storks flew over our heads and we heard the flapping of their wings. As I was writing this I felt penitent and sad, and then, thinking of our time together, suddenly happy. I have been fortunate.

"I want the last word," you say firmly.

Once upon a time there were two sisters who were both called Rose White. This was doubly confusing as they were identical twins, and when anyone called them, they would both answer. Sometimes only one would answer and then she would get the blame or the praise for whatever the other one had done, or at times for what she had done herself. They didn't really mind, but the people around them were bothered. "You have the same name," they said. "You look alike. You dress alike. What we want to know is do you think alike?"

"Oh no," replied Rose White. "She is a feminist. I am not. And she says she's a socialist. I do not. What's more, she would let tigers out of their cages, I would not."

"Oh, that's very different," cried the people. "Thank you so much. So then, which of you is which?"

"Oh, we're both us," Rose White smiled.

11

They are Migratory Birds

After your death, life went on. I kept looking for you, wanting to talk with you, though when we used to talk I only asked the same old questions: What did you have for dinner? Which birds did you see? If I tell you the latest news now, do you care about it? Do you want to be told that the politicians are as inept as ever? Does it matter who won which war? Or which particular person was spiteful and which one was not? Perhaps after one dies the future matters as much or as little as the past ever did.

You've dropped out of time. We can try to speak, but the voices are disjunct: mine, of necessity, goes into the future; yours, of necessity, comes from the past. And you might say that's no different from how it was before when we telephoned and our voices had to cross vast land masses and the ocean. Sometimes there was a time lag. And in any case the space each of us inhabited was different – you could never travel to where I was, not even through a wormhole, and I could only make my usual, sporadic appearances. We might as well have been time travellers or space travellers whose paths diverged and then only converged from time to time. Meanwhile, our memories howled through the continuum, as they do now.

If, in the past, we were seldom together, what difference does it make that now we are never together? It does. It makes a difference. Right now, at this moment, I'm at sea – in both senses. But before when I was on a cruise ship, I would spend time trying to take photographs of the flight of birds so that one day we might look at them together. Now I don't. I stop myself, because I know I cannot show them to you.

We could make an assignation, promise each other we will meet on such and such a day at such and such an hour. How would that work?

> If we meet in the dark woods,
> your face pale,
> your form shadowy, merging
> with the trees,
> what would we say?
> You always speak
> with such gentleness and sadness.
> I am, as usual,
> helpless and stupid. "What," I ask,
> "is the right way to grieve?"

There is no point in imagining Elysian Fields, pleasure groves or even a well-stocked paradise in which you could tell me the names of all the birds you recognised and name the ones you didn't.

My mind batters against a blocked door, and it is not so much a space as knowledge I seek. I know I shall never find it. What should we do, the two of us? My darling, you are like Sleeping Beauty or like Snow White in her glass coffin, and it is my problem, isn't it, not yours? You never said that. You would never say it. But how make a future out of strands of conjecture? To this you say, "Isn't that how the future is always made?" It's how it's imagined as we bridge the gap between what was and what has not happened. I'm not at all sure about the distinction between the real and the imaginary. I'll tell you a secret. I think we see what we imagine. You laugh and say, "Perhaps we imagine what we see? The imagined is based on the real." Whatever, I mumble. The two are intermixed. So then this lifelong conversation in which I put words in your mouth, is it permissible? "Only if what I have to say is what I would probably have said," you reply, laughing at me. I subside into silence. For a moment we talked. Don't you see? I cannot help talking with you. You are always with me.

Things happen. I see pictures of birds in a shop window. And I go up to the window to see if you would like them. Then I remember that I cannot show them to you or tell you about them. Or I read about a heat wave blasting through India and I worry about you and hope you'll give up your dislike of air conditioning. Then I remember and the song kicks in: "Fear no more the heat o' the sun, / nor the furious winter's rages; / Thou thy worldly task hast done, / Home art gone, and ta'en thy wages ..." (From *Cymbeline*) Or someone gives us a pavlova and I think how much you like meringues. They make them much better here in the West, I must – no, I need do nothing. But I'm allowed to remember the things you liked – limes, meringues, peaches, Chinese fried rice, fresh, tender peas and every single bird that ever lived (except owls). There's celebration in that – just in the remembering. There's comfort in that. To remember – is that how one deals with grief?

In the old myths Hades tends to be underground, so should we try that?

> There is no morning, noon or night.
>
> The seasons drift.
>
> At that underground station
>
> I am on a train
>
> and speed past fast.

I think I wave.

Do you wave back?

We have been robbed. All I have left is the memory of you. I do not know whether you have been left with anything at all. Can memory assuage? Re-create the past and make it the lived-in present? Of course not, but under my eyes the sea glitters and a bulky cargo ship makes its slow way and I wish I could show it to you, let your fingertips feel the slight sea breeze. We used to sit on the veranda shelling peas, we could sit on the balcony here just as companionably. There is even an empty chair. The emptiness is filled with thinking of you. You changed my life because you were gentle. Little One, my younger sister, perhaps you, after all, were the Stronger One. Even as I grieve, your kindness fills up all that is.

Yesterday's swallow,

the one you never saw,

flutters between

the past and the future.

Why should she not?

They are migratory birds.

Books by Suniti Namjoshi available from Spinifex Press

The Good-Hearted Gardners

What do you do when you fall in love with your next-door neighbour? You peer at each other through a hole in the fence and eventually climb over.

Sybil is a member of The Good-Hearted Gardeners, a Society for Well-Meaning Efforts for the Betterment of Language and the Salvation of the Planet, which her lover, Demo, is allowed to join. It's funded by MI5, who ask them to monetise and weaponise the English language. Soon afterwards they discover that English is even more widespread than anyone had thought. Even the birds and the fish, the cows and the kangaroos can speak it – when they choose. The Good-Hearted Gardeners set about trying to talk to anyone – crows, magpies, robins, goldfish, cows, horses, rats, mice – who will talk to them.

With climate change and technology gone mad, what's in store is a frightening scenario that threatens everyone – humans, animals, plants. Can the headlong rush to extinction be halted?

When the birds, and the cows and the horses and the mice and all the rest come together, much is made possible. But at what cost? Will the planet and its inhabitants be saved?

A comedic allegory for our future.

ISBN 9781922964007

Feminist Fables

The classic title by Suniti Namjoshi who is both elegant and subversive in creating new patterns of meaning through stories that are simultaneously spare and full of richness. An ingenious reworking of fairy tales from East and West.

ISBN 9781875559190

St Suniti and the Dragon

Where are good and evil to be found? What is the path to sainthood? Is it through poetry or good deeds? St Suniti talks to angels and flowers, dragons, saints and ordinary people in her quest. Suniti Namjoshi has original imagination full of surprises encompassing saints and wolves, Beowulf and Bangladesh, Grendel and Star Trek.

ISBN 9781875559183

Building Babel

Every retelling of a myth is a reworking of it. Every hearing or reading of a myth is a recreation of it. It is only when we engage with a myth that it resonates, becomes charged and recharged with meaning. And so it is in *Building Babel*, a book that re-engages with myth through the cyberworld, where worlds intersect and are transformed.

ISBN 9781875559565

Goja

Suniti Namjoshi traverses the cultures of the East and of the West. She muses on the patterns of her life, and of the impact of colonisation, both the resistances and the acceptances of it. Growing up in the ruling house of Maharashtra, the two most important relationships in her life were with her grandmother, the Ranisaheb, and with Goja, the servant woman who slept beside her bed. Then she moved to the West. In the US and Canada, she became just another brown-skinned immigrant without the privileges of her childhood.

ISBN 9781875559978

The Fabulous Feminist

It was on a sabbatical in England in the late 1970s that Suniti Namjoshi discovered feminism – or rather, she discovered that other feminists existed, and many among them shared her thoughts and doubts, her questions and visions. This collection brings together in one volume a huge range of Namjoshi's writings, starting with her classic collection, *Feminist Fables*, and her later work.

ISBN 9781742198217

Blue and Other Stories

Illustrated by Nilima Sheikh

Suniti Namjoshi, internationally acclaimed fabulist and poet, brings both depth and lightness of touch to *Blue and Other Stories*. Playful and gentle, each of these stories effectively traverses layers of myth to speak to both children and adults.

ISBN 9781742198392

Suki

In *Suki*, Suniti Namjoshi weaves a witty and delightful tapestry from threads of longing, loss, memory, metaphor, and contemplation. *Suki* is a lightly fictionalised memoir of one woman and her cat.

ISBN 9781742198880

Aesop the Fox

Aesop's fables are brought to life by the timely intervention of Sprite from the future, who prods Aesop into debate about the meaning of stories: are they for fun, or do they have the chance to change the world? This book offers a virtuoso display into how the building blocks of fables can enchant, enrage, enlighten and educate us all.

ISBN 9781925581515

If you would like to know more about
Spinifex Press, write to us for a free catalogue, visit our
website or email us for further information
on how to subscribe to our monthly newsletter.

Spinifex Press
PO Box 105
Mission Beach QLD 4852
Australia

www.spinifexpress.com.au

women@spinifexpress.com.au